INNOVATIVE
OFFICE DESIGN

LINKS

INNOVATIVE OFFICE DESIGN

Edition 2013

Author: Carles Broto

Editorial coordination: Jacobo Krauel

Graphic design & production: Xavier Broto & Oriol Vallès

Cover design: Oriol Vallès, graphic designer

Collaborators: Clara Sola

Text: Contributed by the architects, edited by Emily McBride

© **LinksBooks**

Jonqueres, 10, 1-5

08003 Barcelona, Spain

Tel.: +34-93-301-21-99

info@linksbooks.net

www.linksbooks.net

INNOVATIVE
OFFICE DESIGN

LINKS

INDEX

INTRODUCTION

The work environment, as a space for professional and interpersonal exchange, has undergone dramatic changes in recent years. The continued growth in developments in communication technology, resulting in a timeless, ubiquitous and portable handling of information, has greatly contributed to these changes. Gone are the bulky filing cabinets and expansive tables of yester-year, with work surfaces having been reduced to the size of a computer. Tele-work and video-conferencing have also become the norm in many modern workplaces.

At the same time there is an ever-increasing trend towards sustainability in architecture, as evidenced by energy-saving measures, alternative energy sources and the use of new materials.

These, and a host of additional concerns particular to office design, greet the architect and interior designer when drawing up the plans for a new workspace. The company's corporate identity, for example, must be somehow translated into the design both of the interior spaces, and building as a whole. The modern office also requires versatility and dynamism – it must be flexible enough to quickly adapt to a range of uses. It must be aesthetically pleasing and should encourage interpersonal communication among employees, whilst significantly lessening outdated hierarchical barriers.

This volume, which brings together a wide range of examples of renovated spaces as well as new build projects, comprises an invaluable source of inspiration and an in-depth study of the challenges involved in creating new workspaces.

Office Design Guidelines

The debates between open-plan and cellular spaces, private versus collective spaces, are still at the forefront of office design. Today it is generally assumed that a fluid spatial distribution promotes communication within the company, though it is still too early to talk of the disappearance of cellular offices. At the same time, ICT (Information and Communication Technology) advances are bringing about a radical change in the way people work: individual space has reduced thanks to ever smaller and more integrated appliances and flatscreen monitors that have enabled the depth of desks to be reduced. Wireless technology enables ways of working that are more mobile and less tied to a physical space, while at the same time working from home during part of the working day is becoming increasingly popular and viable. These factors together with the provision of more space in offices for meetings and collective working mean that people are spending ever less time in front of their desks. This has led to a new concept in offices, where hierarchy has given way to flexibility and modularity.

DESIGN OF THE BUILDING

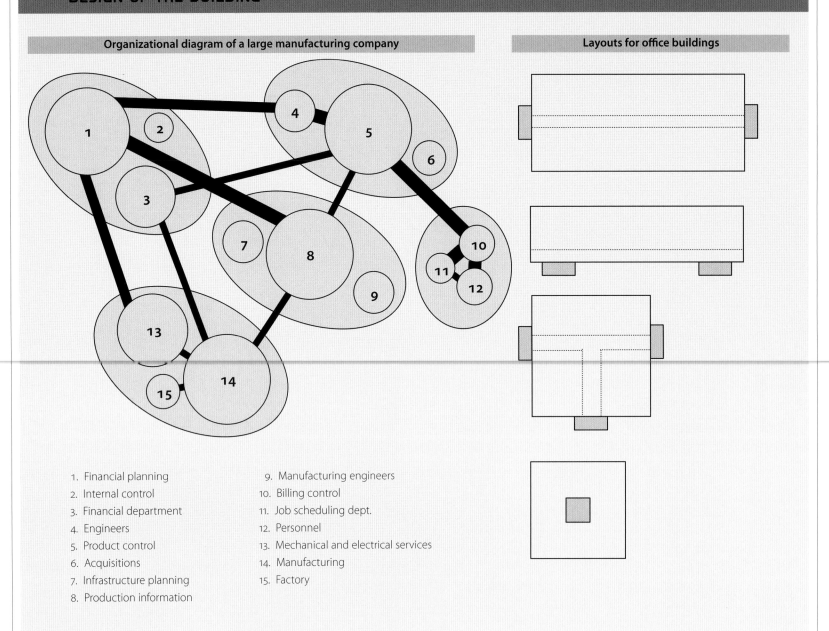

Organizational diagram of a large manufacturing company

Layouts for office buildings

1. Financial planning
2. Internal control
3. Financial department
4. Engineers
5. Product control
6. Acquisitions
7. Infrastructure planning
8. Production information
9. Manufacturing engineers
10. Billing control
11. Job scheduling dept.
12. Personnel
13. Mechanical and electrical services
14. Manufacturing
15. Factory

The optimal dimensions for an office building are dictated by the location and the incidence of natural light. Generally, a good width is accepted to be 5 to 7.5 meters and a height 2 to 2.5 times the width. The depth of the space should ideally be less than 15 meters to guarantee effective passive ventilation, while depths less than 13 meters are incompatible with open-plan or mixed office layouts. Internal atria are often incorporated with the objective of ensuring the incidence of natural light to the center of the building but are incompatible with certain office layouts.

Both the depth of the building and the modulation of the façades should be adapted to the office model, from the traditional modular office to mixed models of the "business club" model for flexible working systems.

While steel structure are well suited to office buildings with rectangular floor plans or of very large area, concrete structures are efficacious in square plan buildings and with relatively small areas. The rational integration of all building elements is essential, from exterior walls to structural elements, ceilings, floors, partition walls, etc. The positioning of windows and vertical load-bearing elements are the most critical factors since they determine the size and position of the partitions. It is preferable that the column spacing is as wide as possible.

It is also preferable that the elevators, stairs and washrooms are concentrated in a single point, in the center of the building, although a large central area and one or two smaller areas in the perimeter of the floor is a viable alternative. The position of these elements strongly conditions the use of the building and its subdivision in different spaces. Placing the stairs, elevators and washrooms in the center of the plan enables a single floor to be divided between different companies although it also limits the conversion of the floor into a single open-plan space.

Spatial typologies and working modes

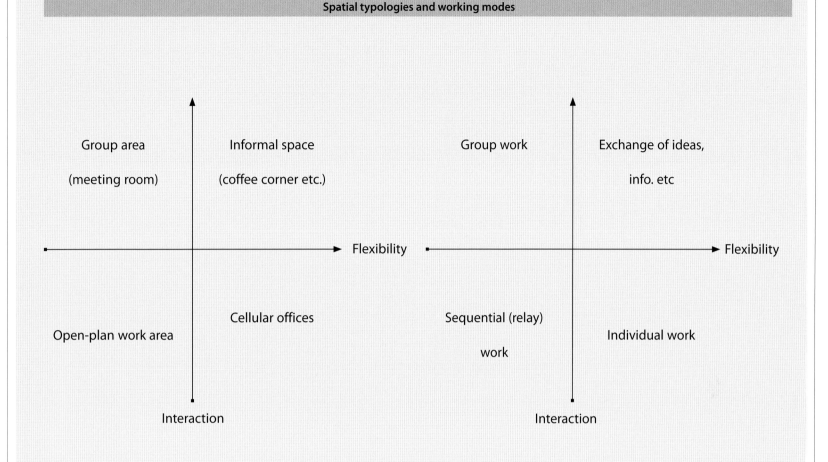

A principle consideration in designing office spaces is the intention to create a building with a long life in a rapidly changing context. As such, the first and most important point is that they need to be **flexible spaces** that can be easily adapted to the demographic, functional, hierarchical and technological changes in companies.

The second fundamental aspect is **communication**, above all informal communication. Although there are no clearly defined spaces for this type of communication, since by the nature of the spontaneity of the interaction they are not designable, they can be consciously cultivated through a successful spatial distribution. The way of connecting individual workspaces and distributing circulation flows influences communication processes and the exchange of information. It should also be taken into account that new ICT infrastructure and knowledge management allow information and data to flow between people without the need for physical proximity.

The most common classification is still that of the **cellular office layout** (where individual workspaces are physically segregated); **open-plan** (with the minimum vertical barriers and organized in work groups); **combined** (a mixed solution containing both open and closed spaces) and the so-called **landscape office**, a sort of business club, without walls, with a free and creative spatial distribution, that combines areas for work, exchanging information, meetings and relaxation.

Relation between working modes and spaces

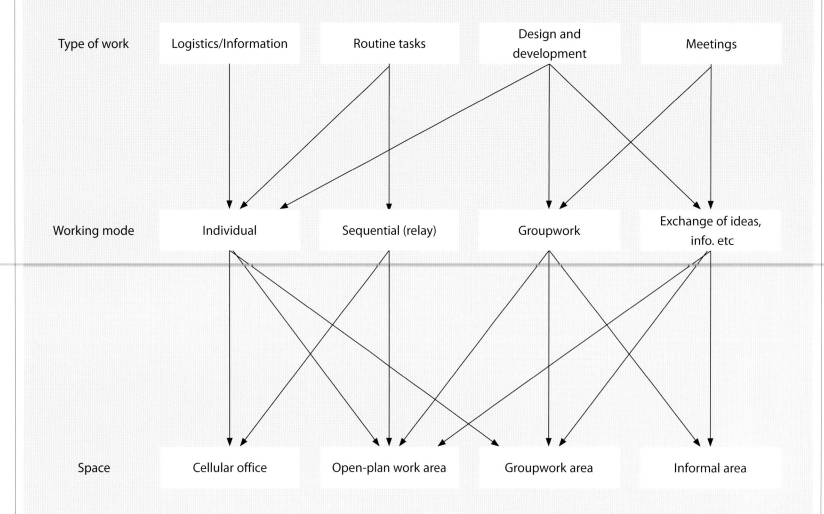

However the spaces are distributed, the ideal proportion of each function, in relation with the net surface area of the office to be the following:
• 50 % for individual workstations arranged in work groups or not.
• 20 % for support spaces for individual work, such as archives, photocopying and printing areas, areas for group work, storage spaces etc.
• 20 % for collective areas for working and relaxing such as meeting or conference rooms, kitchens and washrooms.
• Up to 10 % of the space will not enter into the calculation of usable space, according to the configuration of the building or as consequence of the distribution of the work groups.

An acceptable ratio is around 80 % of the total floor area occupied by work spaces (excluding stairs, elevators and washrooms). Within this 80 % no more than 15 % should be occupied by primary circulation spaces (the routes that connect the principal entrances with the different departments).

Optimal workstation design

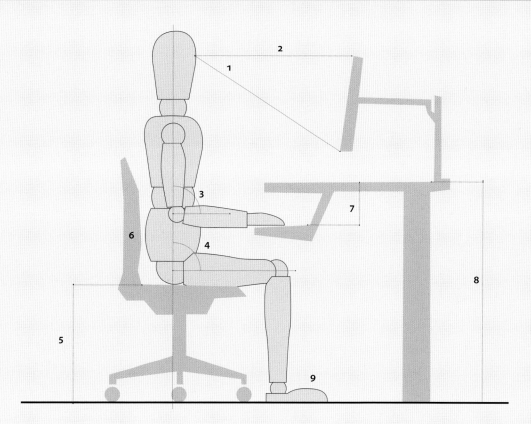

1. Angle of vision for screen: 20°
2. Upper edge of screen at eye level or lower. Distance from eye at arm's length (approx. 42-50 cm (17"-20"))
3. Forearm horizontal or lower (90°-110°)
4. Thighs horizontal or lower (90°-110°)
5. Adjustable seat height (average 42-50 cm (17"-20"))
6. Chair back adjustable in height and tilt, provides firm lower back support
7. Keyboard at 5-10 cm (2" - 4") lower than table surface.
8. Table surface at 65-75 cm (26"- 30") height
9. Feet must rest horizontally on floor or foot rest with ample space under table

THE WORKSTATION

The **individual workstation**, essentially comprised of a table, a chair and the necessary circulation space, is the **basic module** of office design and serves as much for conventional office plans as for more interactive working spaces. The delimitation of the workstation is key to communication at the heart of the company, since it is determinant in the creation of work "neighborhoods" and a team ethos.

The area occupied by one person is calculated at 9 sqm (100 sqft), of which a significant proportion is occupied by the work table and the rest by secondary space, including circulation. The surface area per employee invariably includes a part of the common spaces, such as meeting rooms, and lounges.

The area of the workstation itself ranges from 2.5 sqm to 6 sqm (27 - 65 sqft) per person. The average occupation of offices of 60 sqm (650 sqft) and above is 6 sqm (65 sqft) per person or 7 sqm (75 sqft) in the case of cellular office layouts.

Furniture for an office reception area

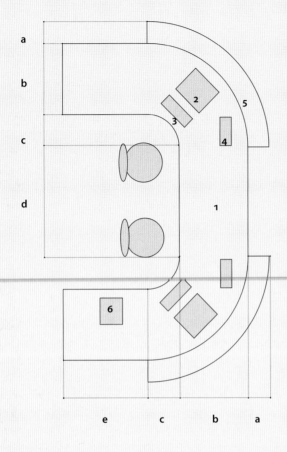

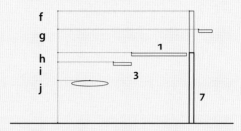

1. Desk
2. Computer screen
3. Keyboard
4. Printer
5. Reception counter
6. Security screen
7. Non-transparent backboard to desk (hides receptionists' feet and computer cables)

a. Counter for visitors: 200 - 250 mm (8" - 10")
b. Table: 600 - 750 mm (2' - 2 1/2')
c. Radius 300 - 400 mm (1' - 1' 4")
d. Desk width: 900 - 1100 mm (3' - 3' 7")
e. Length of side of desk: 700 - 900 mm (2' 4" - 3')
f. Screen height off floor: 1000 - 1200 mm (3' 3" - 4')
g. Counter height: 1000 - 1050 mm (3' 3" - 3' 5")
h. Desk height: 700 - 750 mm (2' 4" - 2 1/2')
i. Keyboard height: 580 - 700 cm (1' 11" - 2' 4")
j. Seat height: 350 - 500 mm (1' 2" - 1' 8")

RECEPTION AND ENTRANCE SPACES

The reception area has become the heart of many companies, the space where the corporate image and brand identity are most intensely expressed. These areas can also accelerate or slow down the flow of employees and forment informal exchanges. They are spaces where square footage is not economized, but rather they are designed as places in which employees can pause and establish contact between one another. A recent tendency is for the concentration of functions in the reception area that go beyond their traditional remit of welcoming and directing visitors. It is an ideal place for establishing relationships, giving rise to the location of small meeting rooms off the reception space for use not only by visitors but also by internal staff.

The entrances can be located in the center of the building, off-center or in a line. Office buildings with off-center entrances often have linear floor plans (well suited to individual, autonomous working) or in a comb formation (ideal for organizations with large groups or departments). Extensions between the wings in the latter case can generate communication spaces between departments.

Centralized entrances are typical of buildings with a circular distribution or a star-shaped distribution that radiates from a central communal circulation space.

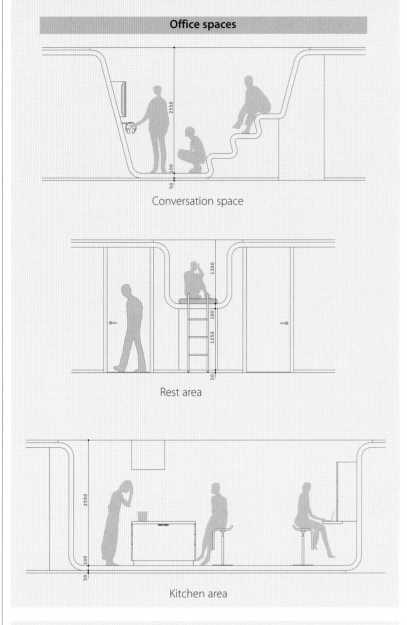

Office spaces

Conversation space

Rest area

Kitchen area

REST AND RELAXATION AREAS

The new work culture gives great importance to areas for rest and relaxation within the workplace. They may contain vending machines, small kitchens and coffee-making facilities in an attractive environment, the visibility of which will attract users. It is positive for the furniture and the décor to mark the difference of this space form the rest of the building, to create an atmosphere that Is completely different form that of the work areas. Special attention should be given to the selection of the furniture and the design of the lighting and acoustics for these spaces, and they should be well ventilated.

In some office buildings, the cafeteria has acquired an essential role as an area for relaxation and is designed not only as a food zone, but also as a space for informal meetings and even individual work.

Another essential space is the staff kitchen or a place where staff can heat food brought from home and do some simple food preparation. This space should be well ventilated and have hardwearing surfaces, appropriate furniture and a series of equipment that will make It a useful area.

MEETING ROOMS

It is becoming more common for different companies that share the same building to use the same meeting rooms. This strategy has a double advantage: it saves space and reduces costs. Open meeting spaces that occupy less room and combine an area for group work with a lounge space are also becoming common. Small closed meeting rooms, from four people, are generally the most useful for meetings that do not involve audiovisual presentations, while **meeting "islands"** (furnished with sofas, coffee tables and stools) and used by all staff for informal and formal communication are a modern alternative to the traditional meeting room with a central table.

COLLECTIVE WORK SPACES

Complementary modules or additional computer stations complement the basic work stations. They are specialized or monofunctional spaces for occasional use, and may provide services such as high-end CAD or multimedia software or be places with special characteristics such as reflection zones. The articulation of meeting spaces and communal areas facilitates exchange between different work groups, so such spaces should be placed in strategic points, for example, alongside principal circulation spaces where they are accessible to everyone. They should be semi-public in character while offering the possibility for more private discussion.

RESTROOMS

This is a key space in an office building, since its location is usually predetermined. The restrooms form part of a group of facilities that, like the stairs and elevators, have an important influence on the distribution of the office, since all users of the building must have easy access and be practically equidistant from these spaces.

The minimum dimensions of an accessible toilet are 2 x 1.5 meters. Doors should also open outwards and, in the case of them opening inwards, sufficient space should be allowed for the door leaf and for the user to open and shut it. Adapting a toilet for wheelchair users requires the toilet and hand basin to be changed, a wider door to be fitted and the installation of security handrails on walls with a sufficient loading capacity.

Special attention should be given critical aspects such as anti-slip floor surfaces; the installation of buttons, faucets and handles within reaching distance of a wheelchair user and control of the water temperature. Electronic faucets which detect the presence of a hand beneath them, are gradually replacing timer faucets, for their convenience, hygiene (the user does not touch the device) and their greater water consumption efficiency.

Types of stairs

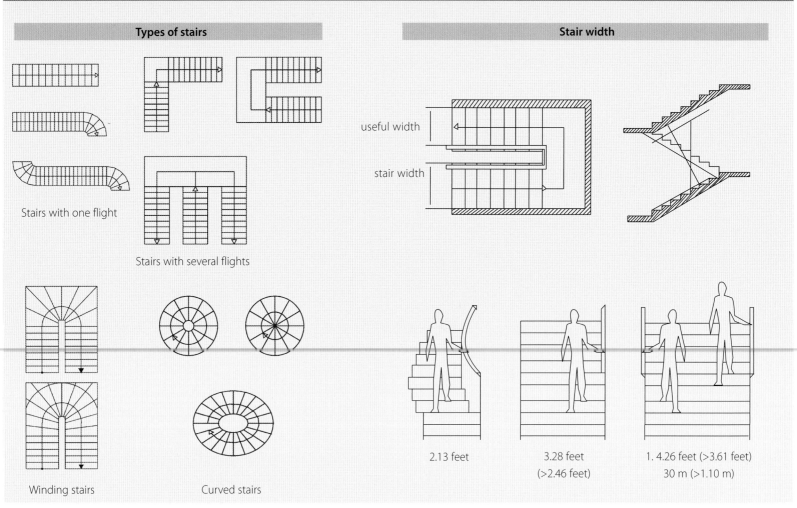

Stairs with one flight

Stairs with several flights

Winding stairs

Curved stairs

Stair width

useful width

stair width

2.13 feet

3.28 feet
(>2.46 feet)

1. 4.26 feet (>3.61 feet)
30 m (>1.10 m)

Primary circulation spaces are those that define the most important routes in the building, connecting the principal spaces in the building with the different departments; and secondary circulation spaces that connect the individual workspaces. The way in which people move through the building affects how they interact and relate to each other.

Although staircases can resolve the circulation of large volumes of people, they are inefficient in terms of the area they occupy and their cost. This means that they are often placed at strategic points in office buildings, to facilitate the movement of certain large groups or to connect the first floor and the ground floor.

Elevators should be able to move at least 15% of the workforce in a period of 5 minutes, with a maximum waiting time of 30 seconds. For buildings of more than 10,000 sqm (108,000 sqft) a separate service elevator should be installed.

In offices distributed over various floors, the vertical circulation between each floor is realized via stairs and elevators. The latter are indispensable as they enable wheelchair users and other reduced-mobility users to navigate the building. As in the case of corridors and doors, the dimensions of a wheelchair should be considered when choosing the elevator model.

Staircases are elements that mark the design of a space. They are fixed elements that determine the distribution of the offices. There are many different designs of staircase: straight stairs, those that change direction between flights, compensated stairs and curved stairs.

The form and style of a staircase is also determined by the construction materials chosen: stone or concrete will give a more monumental appearance, while glass or plastic can be used to achieve more minimalist designs.

The width of a staircase is defined by its limits, but it is often reduced at the sides by a banister or string. The useful width of a staircase is thus defined as the span between the two handrails or between the handrail and the wall.

The width of stairs is also determined by the number of persons who must circulate in both directions, by the time in which a building must be evacuated and by the importance of the building in which they are located. According to the number of persons that use the stairs, they are classified as follows:

- For 1 person   2.13 feet (minimum 1.15)
  (Winding stair or narrow straight stair)
- For 1 person   3.28 feet (minimum 2.46)
- For 2 persons   4.26 feet (minimum 3.61)
- For 3 persons   6.23 feet (minimum 5.90)

Doors and switches

Minimum space requirements for hinged doors

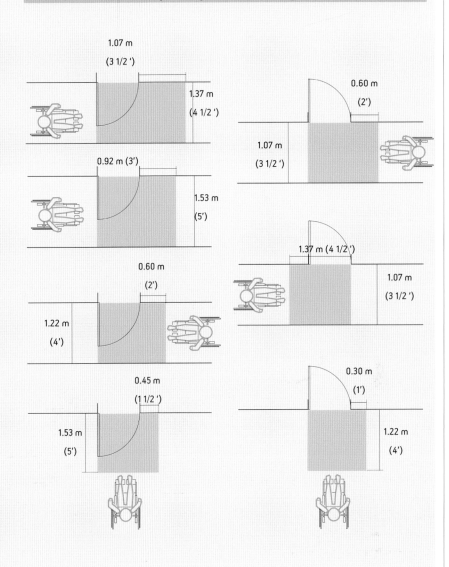

1. Height 900-1000 mm (3'- 3' 3"). Handles and switches should be aligned at this height.
2. 400 mm (1' 4") high protection panel in doors.
3. Maximum and minimum heights for control elements: 600 mm (2'); 1200 mm (4').

All public buildings should be fitted with control panels and signage designed for users with reduced mobility and installed within the standard reach of a wheelchair user: up to 1220 mm (4') from the finished floor level for depths of up to 510 mm (20") , and 1120 mm (3'8") from the F.F.L. for depths of up to 635 mm (25") when the device is accessed from the front. When the wheelchair user can access the device laterally their reach is from 380 mm (15") to 1370 mm (4-1/2') above the F.F.L.

All control panels should fulfil three conditions: they should be installed at an accessible height, easy to use (they should be easy to hold, non-slip and require minimal force in their manipulation), while information should be easy to read and comprehend (large lettering and clear communication). Electronic controls can resolve many accessibility barriers presented by elements such as windows, blinds and doors.

Stairlifts are a space-efficient alternative to ramps for small changes of level. Incorporating either a seat or a platform for the wheelchair user, **stairlifts** can cover large distances and even be fitted in staircases with various flights and changes in direction. They are an ideal solution for improving the accesibility of existing buildings, although the building regulations prohibit their installation on stairs in emergency evacuation routes.

The main entrance should serve both able-bodied and reduced-mobility users. The most practical door type are two-leaf automatic sliding doors with detectors that ensure that they will only shut once the user has passed right through the doorway. Rotating and pivoting doors are not recommendable and any door that requires the user to open it physically should be avoided.

Dimensions of the human body

Wheelchair dimensions

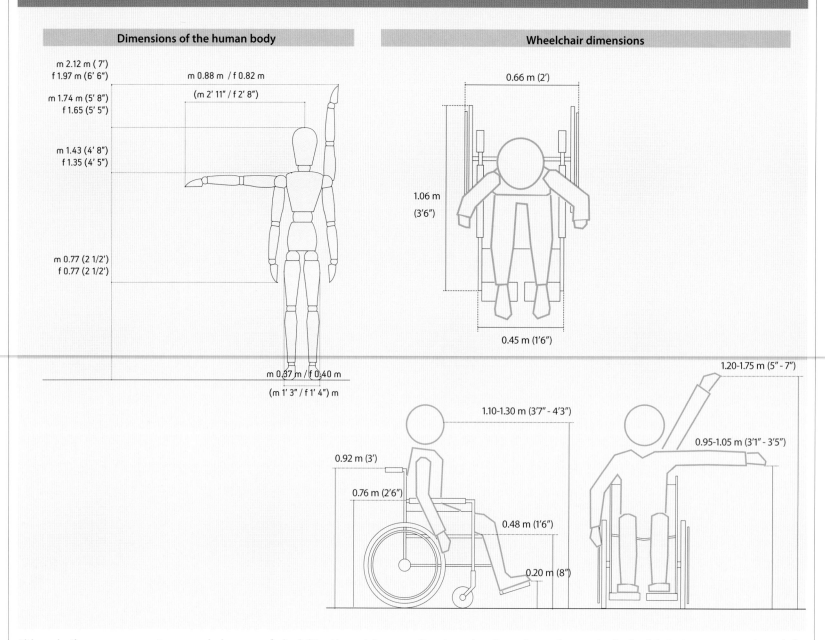

Although there are many types and degrees of disability, the minimum requirement for a public building is adaptation to the needs of a user in a wheelchair since this condition requires certain adaptations of the built environment that are assumed to make the building more functional for those with other types and degrees of disability.

There are essentially three components to consider in a project for improving the accessibility of an existing building: increasing the width of doors and circulation spaces; inserting additional elevators and ramps to reduce circulation distances and ensure access to all levels can be achieved without using stairs; the use of appropriate mechanical apparatus and new technologies to increase comfort.

Based on the dimensions of a standard wheelchair, its turning circle and the standard reach of a wheelchair user, the building regulations for accessibility define dimensions for room widths, doorways, corridors, the height of switches, taps, telephones, and control panels. People with reduced mobility need more space than other people. While the minimum area for an individual workstation is around 4 sqm (43 sqft), a wheelchair user will need around 5 or 6 sqm (54 - 65 sqft).

A wheelchair user needs a minimum unobstructed width of 915 mm (3ft 2 in) when moving forwards in a straight line, and a circle with a diameter of 1525 mm (5 ft) to turn the chair. In general, 1.3 meters (4 ft 3 in) has been established as the standard width of corridors.

Changes in the floor level of more than 13 mm (5 in) should be accompanied by a ramp, while level changes between 6 and 13 mm (2 and 5 in) should be resolved without a step, by connecting the two floor heights with a continuous sloping plane no steeper than 45 °. Ramps should be straight, with a gradient no greater than 7 % and a length of less than 6 meters (20 ft).

ACCESSIBILITY

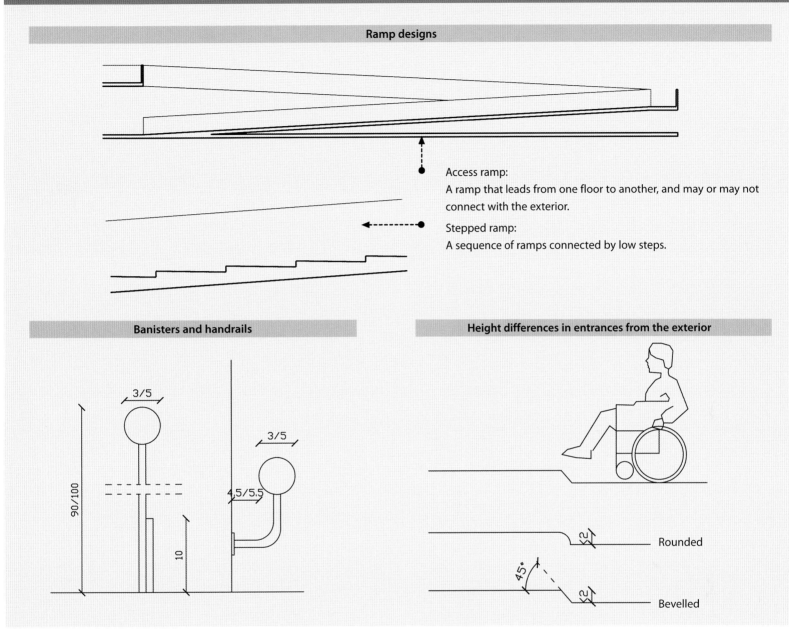

Ramp designs

Access ramp:
A ramp that leads from one floor to another, and may or may not connect with the exterior.

Stepped ramp:
A sequence of ramps connected by low steps.

Banisters and handrails

3/5

3/5

90/100

10

4,5/5,5

Height differences in entrances from the exterior

Rounded

45°

Bevelled

The unobstructed width of the ramp must be greater than or equal to 1.2 m (4 ft) and it must be equipped with a handrail that accompanies the its full length and continues beyond its beginning and end, which are considered critical points. Ramps that are especially wide should be fitted with a double central handrail.

A ramp, defined as an inclined plane that connects two levels at different heights, is the element that allows uneven ground to become accessible to all. The design of a ramp is a basic element for accessibility, but the way it is implemented is also important and regular maintenance is required to ensure that the element does not deteriorate. A ramp should be protected as much as possible from environmental agents and lit at night.

Details of brick or blockwork partition walls

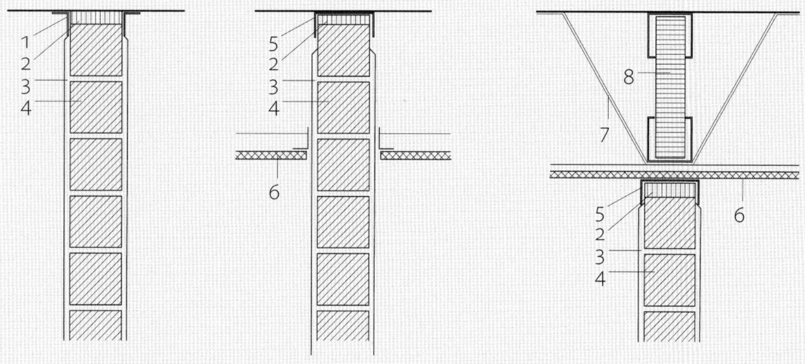

1. Steel angle
2. Rockwool
3. Plaster
4. Brick / blockwork
5. Steel U-section
6. False ceiling
7. Suspension elements
8. Insulation

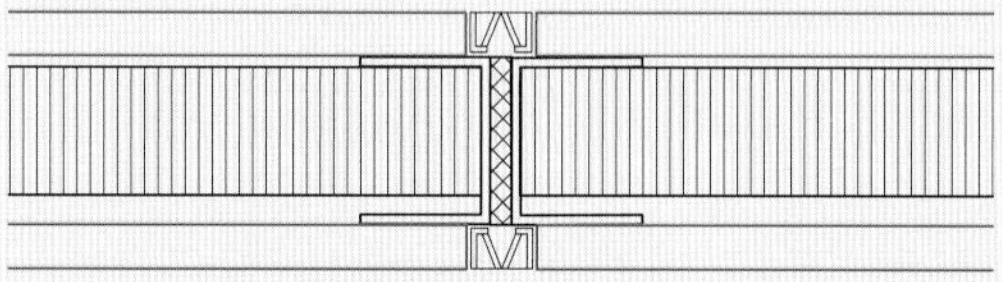

Expansion joint

Double leaf partition for greater acoustic insulation

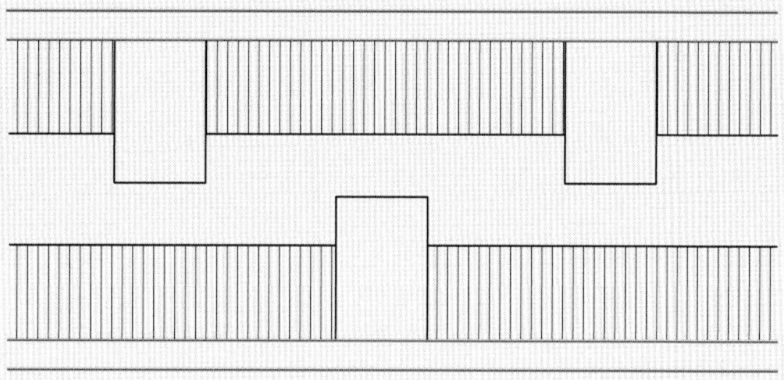

Armstrong suspended ceiling systems

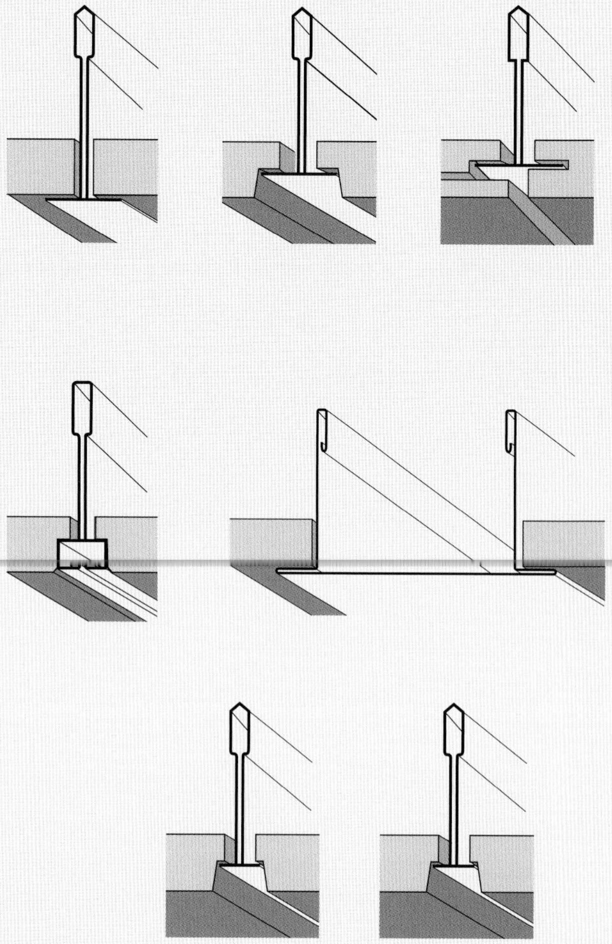

PARTITIONS

Limits between different areas can be marked by different elements - with freestanding partitions or walls - or simply left implicit in the distribution of the furniture. Partitions can be **fixed or movable**, the latter being particularly relevant for auditoriums or conference rooms. The function if the partition is as much to attenuate noise as it is to create visual privacy. Movable partitions can be quickly and easily installed and removed, and there are models available that are designed with high acoustic specifications. They are however more expensive than fixed partitions, have a shorter lifespan and are less effective as fire barriers and acoustic barriers than plasterboard, ceramic or brick partitions.

CEILINGS

False, or suspended, ceilings reduce the height of the space by around 140 mm when they are used to house lighting fittings, smoke detectors, cabling and sprinklers. Acoustic panels fixed on lightweight metallic substructures are the most common solution. They are available in a wide range of sizes and finishes and with a great variety of fixing systems. Cabling and fittings installed within the ceiling void should be easily accessible.

Types of flooring

1. Ceramic tiles
2. Tiling mortar
3. Concrete slab
4. Waterproof barrier (2 layers)
5. Insulation
6. Fill strip
7. Elastic sealant
8. Skirting board
9. Parquet
10. OSB board
11. Cellulose panel
12. Mineral board
13. Anti-capillary layer
14. Composite timber board
15. Wooden board
16. Timber joist
17. Reinforced concrete
18. Glass bricks
19. Support
20. Elastic seal
21. Expansion joint

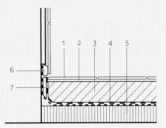

Ceramic tiles on concrete slab

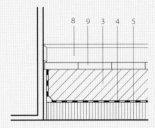

Wooden parquet on concrete slab

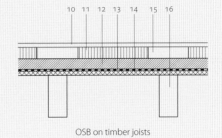

OSB on timber joists

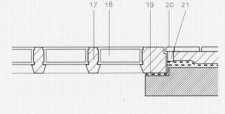

Glass brick floor (max. dimensions 3.50 × 1.60 m)

FLOORING

The ideal floor to ceiling height is 2.6 to 3 meters (8-1/2' - 10'), so when specifying the installation of **technical floors**, the finished floor level should be taken into account. Technical floors are generally installed at a height of 150 mm (6") above the floor slab, although they can be as high as 200 or 250 mm (8" - 10") in special cases and can even be 450 mm (18") high if they contain ventilation ducts and air-conditioning conduits. These flooring solutions, that are invariably very difficult to install in historic buildings, should be defined according to a series of considerations, such as the strength of the floor structure and the correct distribution of supports so that the loading will not become uneven if the applied loads increase or are redistributed. The under floor area should be easy to access for maintenance and replacement of cabling and other elements. Vertical fire barriers should be installed in the under floor area to prevent the propagation of fire.

The choice of **flooring material** will depend on various factors: not only its appearance and the company's corporate image, but also the cost, health and safety, durability, and the ease of maintenance and installation. There is a wide range of options, from ceramic tiles to carpet, laminated flooring or parquet, linoleum and vinyl or even metallic floors.

Light color and temperature for various spaces

	Skywhite	Cool daylight		Daylight	Cool white		White	Warm white	Extra warm white
color name:	Skywhite	Cool daylight		Daylight	Cool white		White	Warm white	Extra warm white
color code:	880	865	965	954	840	940	835	830	835
color temperature:	8000 K	6500 K	6500 K	5400 K	4000 K	4000 K	3500 K	3000 K	3500 K
Offices, corridors	✓				✓		✓	✓	
Meeting rooms	✓						✓	✓	✓
Electrical industry		✓			✓				
Textile industry		✓	✓	✓					
Woodworking industry		✓	✓	✓	✓				
Graphics industry, laboratories		✓	✓	✓	✓				
Color matching			✓	✓		✓			
Warehouses, transport depots					✓				

Typical luminance values (cd/m²)	
The Sun	1 650 000 000
Incandescent lamp	7 000 000
Fluorescent lamp	8 000
Full moon	2 500

Typical illuminance values (lx)	
Sunny day	80 000
Overcast day	5 000
Table lamp	300
Ceiling lamp	100
Full moon	0,1

Conversions for units of temperature			
	into Fahrenheit	into Celsius	into Kelvin
from Fahrenheit	F	$(°F - 32)/1,8$	$(°F - 32) \times 5/9 + 273,15$
from Celsius	$(°C \times 1,8) + 32$	C	$°C + 273,15$
from Kelvin	$(K - 273,15) \times 9/5 + 32$	$K - 273,15$	K

The internal environment of the workplace affects how people work. It has been demonstrated that in uncomfortable temperature or lighting conditions productivity is reduced, while noise reduces concentration levels. The current trend is towards healthier, more cost efficient and more environmentally sustainable working environments.

Psychologists have also shown that being able to control the **comfort** conditions of their immediate environment (for example being able to open the windows) gives workers a positive perception of their work station.

The **ventilation** is one of the most critical aspects in the design of an office, since users invariably value natural ventilation through windows above any mechanical system, however efficient or healthy it may be.

Floor depths of less than 15 meters (50') are optimal for natural ventilation, but buildings narrower than 13 meters (43') become difficult to distribute with open-plan offices in combination with enclosed work spaces. The ideal solution is to use a combination of ventilation systems that can accommodate spaces with specific demands such as restrooms, photocopying rooms, laboratories or kitchens. It would be unacceptable for odors from a staff kitchen to spread into work areas.

LIGHTING AND NOISE

Lamp types

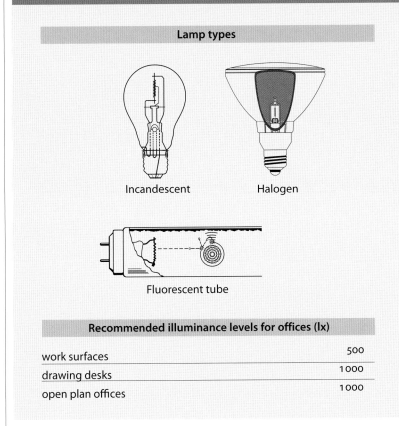

Incandescent

Halogen

Fluorescent tube

Human hearing

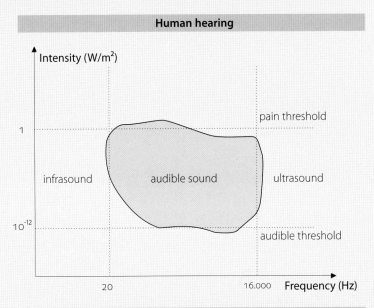

Recommended illuminance levels for offices (lx)

work surfaces	500
drawing desks	1000
open plan offices	1000

Airborne noise (a) impact noise (b)

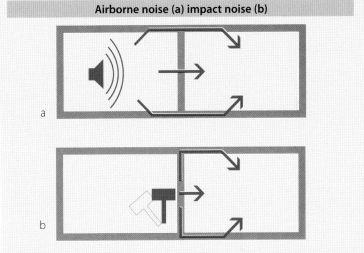

LIGHTING

Lighting is another critical aspect as it directly affects comfort and productivity. The current belief is that visual contact with the exterior is essential for effective working: this is why the façades of office buildings are extensively glazed and workstations are placed close to windows.

The amount of light needed to realize a given task varies from person to person, and especially in function of age: people over sixty need lighting levels with an intensity four times greater than that required by under-twenties, for example.

Natural light is always preferable for workspaces. Daylighting levels depend on the building design and principally on the floor to ceiling height that will determine how far it enters the building. It is considered that spaces lit from only one side should be no deeper than 2.5 times the floor to ceiling height. A distance of up to 7.5 meters (25') is generally acceptable in sunny climates.

Natural light contributes considerably to the **energy efficiency** of the building when daylight levels at the workstations reaches 500 lux and the artificial lighting can be turned off. It is important to remember, however, that the lighting level does not depend only on incident light but also on the reflected light. On very bright days the intensity of the natural light may cause internal lighting conditions with excessive contrast, in which case artificial lighting will need to be used. The possibility of regulating the natural light at their workstation and the intensity and orientation of artificial light is one of the characteristics that users value most highly. Natural light can be controlled and modified using blinds fitted on the eastern, southern and western façades of the building.

NOISE

Noise is the last key design issue and one of the most conflictive in open office spaces: achieving **acoustic privacy** contradicts the visual openness of the space. Walls and partitions are the most effective devices for reducing noise levels, blocking its propagation and absorbing, masking or diffusing sound. There are various suspended ceiling or flooring solutions that are designed to absorb or diffuse airborne sound and impact noise.

Protection against external noise can be improved by installing a double façade, the outer skin acting as an acoustic panel. The effectiveness of this solution depends largely on the size and position of windows and ventilation openings.

The void between the two leaves of the façade can also be used to attenuate sound by fitting it with acousticallly absorbent surfaces. This strategy can achieve an improvement of 3 to 6 decibels in the acoustic insulation of a façade with a window area of 10 % of the total surface area.

Façades. Designing to reduce heating and lighting energy loads.

External ambient
temperature
Air movement
External relative
humidity
Solar radiation
Ambient noise
Precipitation

External factors

Façade - Roof
Heating and air-condi-
tioning systems
Artificial lighting

Control systems

Internal temperature
Air quality
Internal relative humidity
Lighting
Absence of noise

User needs

Points in the façade vulnerable to damp

1

2

4

3

5

In all types of buildings, particularly in office buildings, the façade has evolved from a structural function to a non load-bearing, simple function of enclosure. The envelopes are **lightweight**, thin and multi-layer; and fulfil with greater or lesser efficiency the functions of insulation, water-proofing and air tightness. The façade design determines the natural illumination of the interior, The façade design is key to controlling the daylighting conditions of the interior, managing the solar gains and the natural ventilation to ensure a good air quality and the elimination of excess heat through convection.

The contemporary tendency is for energy consumption and the use of passive strategies to form a key consideration from the earliest stages of the design of the building. The form the building and the façade impact directly on the building's climatic relationship with the surroundings through two principle factors: the surface area – the larger the surface area, the greater the capacity for energy exchange between the interior and exterior.

The independization of the structure from the façade enclosure represents a definitive advance in the process of the increasing autonomy of the façade.

The most universal façade solution in office buildings is the glazed curtain wall. Realized with industrially manufactured components, it is designed to resist wind loads and its own self-weight which is transmitted to the structure of the building through the fixings. This element has to resolve a complex series of problems: the dimensional limits of the glazing lites, the transmission of forces to the building structure, differential movement between the building structure and the curtain wall, etc.

Wind pressure can cause the glazing to flex and even break. This can be controlled by giving the panels sufficient points of support with appropriate spans. The most effective solution is to support the glazing panels on bars that distribute the wind loads and self-weight along their length and are fixed to the floor plates. A continuous façade can be achieved by placing the building envelope outside the plane of the building structure supported on its own substructure such that it is not interrupted by the floor plates. This solution has the advantages of eliminating thermal bridges and reducing the vulnerability to damp.

ENERGY EFFICIENCY ON THE FAÇADE

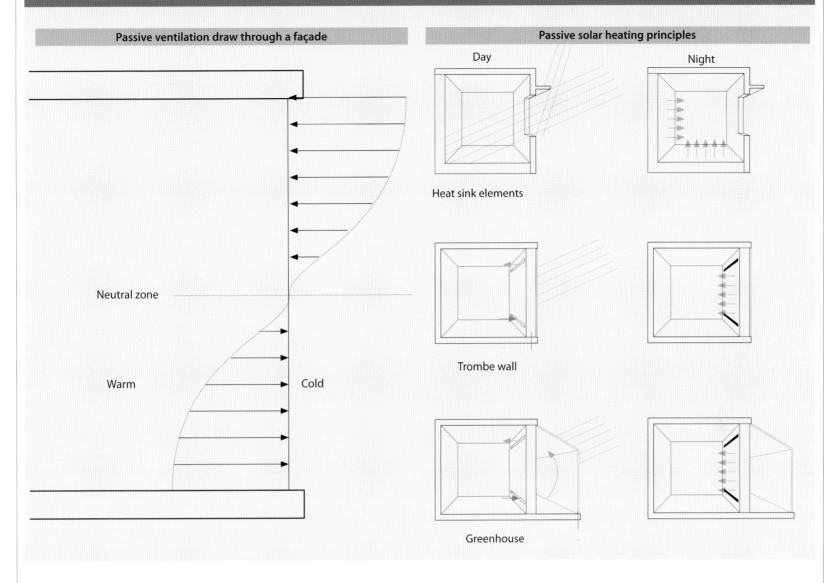

Passive ventilation draw through a façade

Neutral zone

Warm | Cold

Passive solar heating principles

Day | Night

Heat sink elements

Trombe wall

Greenhouse

Another problem is the **thermal expansion** of the building envelope: if the panels and substructure of the façade are independent between floors, the dimensional changes will be minimal, but if the curtain wall is continuous is will need expansion joints.

The solutions to the waterproofing and drainage of the façade as well as its impermeability to water vapor are in the design of the joints of the curtain-walling system: whether those of the frame, between the glazing and the frame or between glazing panels directly. The common design options are elastic sealants, overlapping elements, joint covering elements or the "open joint".

Condensation can occur not only on the surface of the glazing but also on the framing elements. These latter should be thermally broken if they are in contact with exterior and interior air, while the use of low-emissivity glass reduces the energy lost through the glazing. Moisture that has condensed on the inside of the façade or that has filtered through should have means of draining through drainage channels incorporated in the framing elements.

The energy gains and losses through the glazing will be affected by the design of units and the glass, options including the incorporation of translucent insulation, double or triple glazing and the use of special glasses with high reflectivity, low emissivity etc.

A factor that can prove problematic in the use of glazed curtain walls is controlling solar gains, since the greenhouse effect means that the façade allows energy into the building which then cannot radiate back out.

Façade solutions using metal panels are also common in office buildings, the most common being of aluminum and galvanized steel although stainless steel, copper and zinc are also common materials. New materials include plastic panels, used especially in cases with very tight loading constraints and high strength and rigidity demands.

HEAT

Passive solar control elements

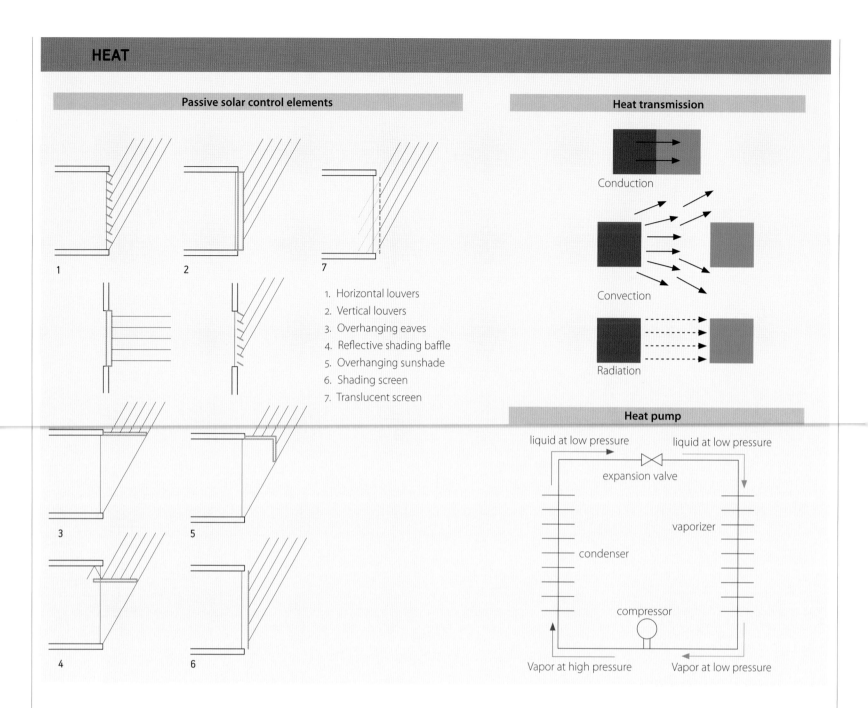

1. Horizontal louvers
2. Vertical louvers
3. Overhanging eaves
4. Reflective shading baffle
5. Overhanging sunshade
6. Shading screen
7. Translucent screen

Heat transmission

Conduction

Convection

Radiation

Heat pump

liquid at low pressure   liquid at low pressure

expansion valve

vaporizer

condenser

compressor

Vapor at high pressure   Vapor at low pressure

The regulation of the internal temperature of an office building should be understood holistically, from the thermal insulation to the heating and air-conditioning systems, while always bearing in mind the use of renewable energies.

Adapting the internal conditions of the building to the local climatic and microclimatic conditions should be a fundamental parameter in the design of the building. Multi-layered façades can offer important advantages, enabling nighttime cooling and reducing pressure fluctuations even when windows are open. Double-layered façades with box windows are an interesting option for renovation projects, allowing the climatic performance of an existing façade to be improved at the same time as giving the façade a whole new appearance.

The universally accepted ideal temperature is 21 °C (70°F) in the summer (up to maximum of 24 °C (75 °F)) and 22 °C (72 °F) in the winter, with a fresh air intake of 8-12 liters per person per second. Large low temperature radiant surfaces are taking over from convection radiators since they operate at lower temperatures (around 30°C (86°F)) and are more energy efficient. Large surfaces are needed to transmit the heat, favoring systems in which the heat source is integrated into the fabric of building, typically in the floor, walls or ceiling.

Mechanical air renovation systems, (supplying 30-50 m³/h (1060-1870 cu.ft)) mean that heat is not lost through open windows, and heat can be recovered from the exhaust air with high efficiency heat-exchangers. The specific requirements of areas such as restrooms, kitchens, laboratories or photocopying rooms should be taken into account in the design of the air systems.

Evacuation routes

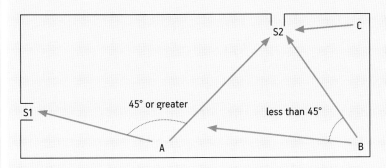

If the escape route starts at point A and separates in two at point B, the angle must be greater than or equal to 45° + 2.5° for each additional meter between A and B.
Point C serves only as an evacuation route.

Point A has two alternative routes because angle S1-A-S2 is 45° or more. Point B hasn't got two alternative routes because angle S1-B-S2 is less than 45°. Point C also has only one evacuation route.

Positioning of protected stair cores and emergency exits

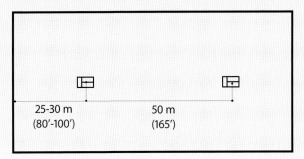

Multistory building with stair cores in the center of the floor plates

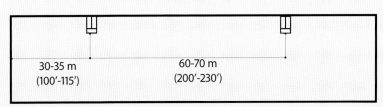

Multistory building with stair cores giving onto a façade

Evacuation routes distances

	One escape route		Two escape routes	
	(m)	(ft)	(m)	(ft)
Offices	18	60'	45	150'
Assembly halls				
a. with fixed seating	15	50'	32[b]	100'
b. without fixed seating	18	60'	45[c]	150'
Storage	18	60'		

a: The evacuation distances for industrial buildings depend on the danger level. In this case a "normal" danger level is assumed.
b: This can be up to 15 meters in one direction.
c: This can be up to 18 meters in one direction.

The building regulations relating to fire safety mark the maximum volume of each fire compartment. This volume can be increased if automatic smoke extraction or sprinkler systems are to be installed and by relocating key elements such as the stairs. The minimum width for evacuation routes is also stipulated along with other criteria, including adequate signage to make the routes easily identifiable by all users of the building.

El punto A dispone de dos vías alternativas de evacuación, dado que el ángulo S1AS2 ≥ 45°.
El punto B no dispone de dos vías alternativas de evacuación, dado que el ángulo S1BS2 < 45°.
El punto C dispone de tan sólo una vía de evacuación

Langarita-Navarro Arquitectos

Red Bull Music Academy

Madrid, Spain

Photographs: contributed by Langarita-Navarro Arquitectos

In many ways, the logic of this project resembles that of a matryoshka doll, not only in the literal sense of one layer being contained within another, but also in a more temporary sense, one aspect or element being born from another.

The Red Bull Music Academy (RMBA) is an annual musical event that has taken place in a different city around the world for the last 14 years. Each year it welcomes 60 participants and surrounds them with musicians, producers and DJs so as to allow experimentation and the exchange of ideas to ferment in a creative atmosphere. Due to the earthquake and subsequent Fukushima disaster, the event which was meant to be the RBMA in Tokyo in 2011 had to quickly change tracks and seek a new home, with less than 5 months notice. Madrid stepped up to the occasion and took the opportunity to recreate the Madrid Slaughterhouse, housed in an early 20th century industrial complex, as a new venue.

The aim was to create, under urgent time pressures, an infrastructure that was able, in addition to responding to specific technical and acoustic conditions, to promote, accelerate and enrich a series of intense artistic relationships between the participating musicians. This in turn was to supply a setting where this could be recorded and archived. Further restrictions were in place as the shell of the slaughterhouse had to be maintained and protected, and the exhibition needed to be temporary, and cause as small a footprint in the host location as possible.

The resulting project unfolds within the slaughterhouse premises as a disjointed urban structure, which, through the variable relationship between closeness and independence, pre-existence and action, is able to provide unforeseen settings for the musical community that inhabits it.

Architecture:
Langarita-Navarro Arquitectos,
María Langarita and Víctor Navarro
Collaborators:
Juan Palencia, Gonzalo Gutierrez, Tonia Papanikolau, Paula García-Masedo
Quantity Surveyor:
Javier Reñones
Landscaper:
Jerónimo Hagerman
Services:
Úrculo ingenieros
Acoustics:
Imar Sanmartí Acousthink S.L.
Structures:
Mecanismo S.L.
Light Structures:
Arquiges y Cuatro50

Ground floor plan

0   10   20

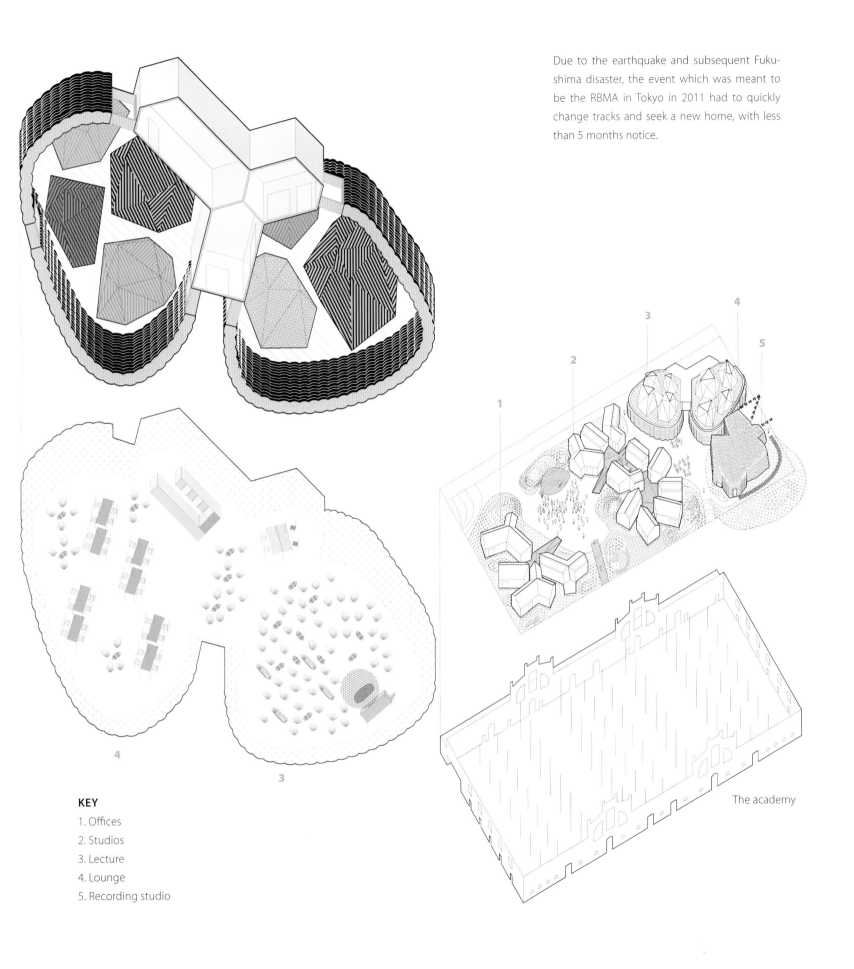

Due to the earthquake and subsequent Fukushima disaster, the event which was meant to be the RBMA in Tokyo in 2011 had to quickly change tracks and seek a new home, with less than 5 months notice.

KEY

1. Offices
2. Studios
3. Lecture
4. Lounge
5. Recording studio

The academy

The festival was finally hosted by the City of Madrid, and housed in the old slaughterhouse, in an early 20th century industrial complex.

The garden

The resulting project unfolds within the slaugh-terhouse premises as a disjointed urban structure, which, through the variable relationship between closeness and independence, pre-existence and action, is able to provide unforeseen settings for the musical community that inhabits it.

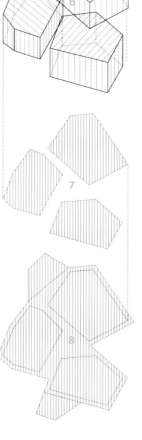

CONSTRUCTION SYSTEM

1. Domes on lattice support structure
2. Sandbag wall
3. Kitchen and radio pavilions, concrete slab
4. Sandbag wall
5. Exterior covering
6. Interior covering
7. Floating slabs
8. Concrete slabs
9. Exterior wood covering
10. Metallic structure
11. Floating slab
12. Support structure

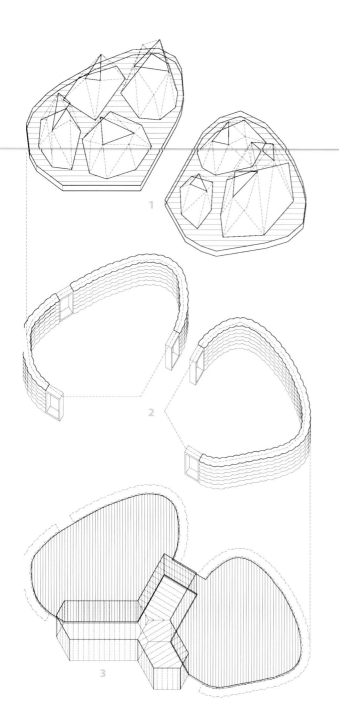

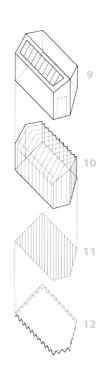

LOUNGE & LECTURE HALL   **RECORDING STUDIO**   **OFFICES STUDIOS**

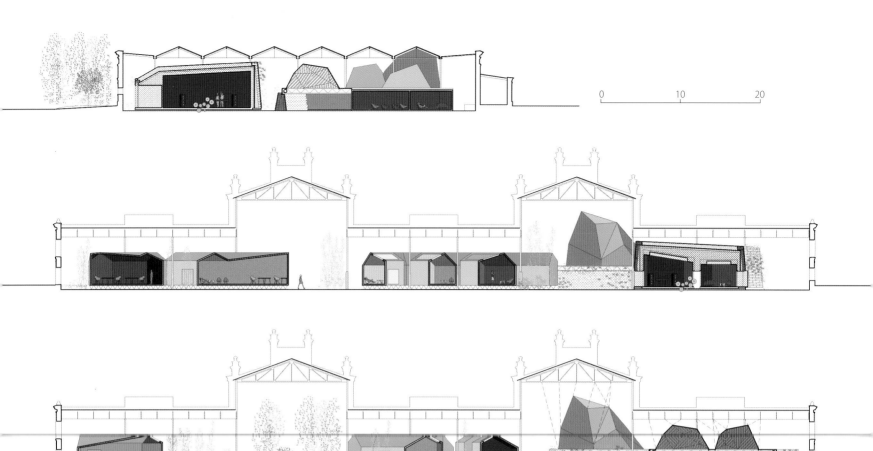

General sections

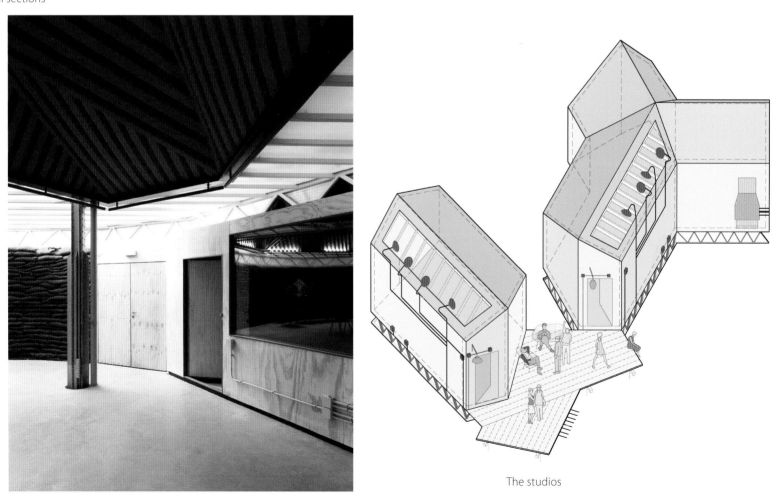

The studios

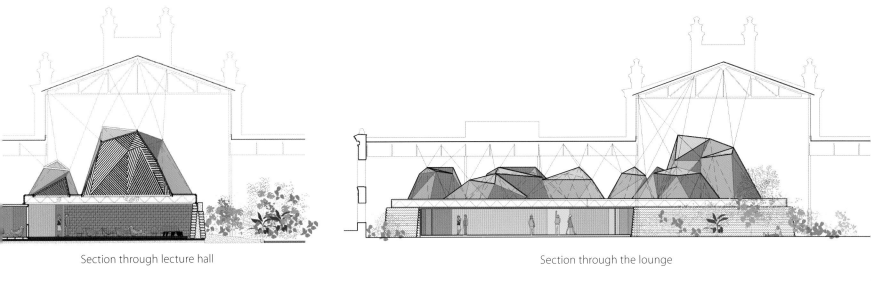

Section through lecture hall

Section through the lounge

RECORDING MOUNTAIN CONSTRUCTION SYSTEM

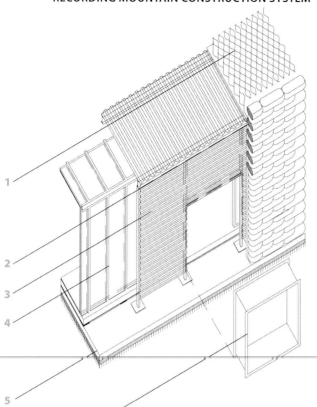

LECTURE HALL CONSTRUCTION SYSTEM

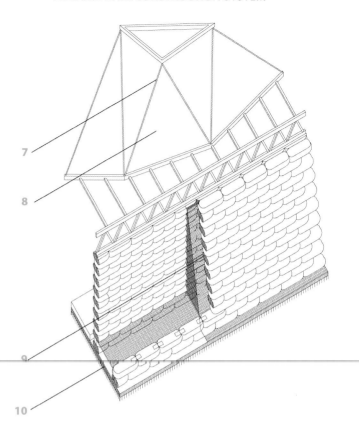

WOOD PAVILIONS CONSTRUCTION SYSTEM

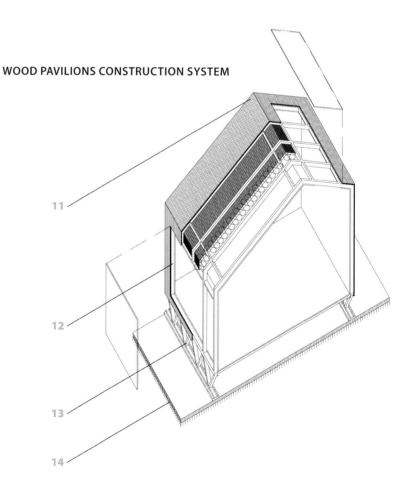

LECTURE HALL CONSTRUCTION SYSTEM

1. Green earth roof
2. Green sandbag wall
3. Exterior cover
4. Interior cover
5. Interior-exterior rooms
6. Foundation and floors
7. Dome structure
8. Dome finishing
9. Green sandbag wall
10. Floor foundations
11. Wood pavilions
12. Doors and hollows
13. Foundation over support structure
14. Site support preparation

The aim was to create, under urgent time pressures, an infrastructure that was able, in addition to responding to specific technical and acoustic conditions, to promote, accelerate and enrich a series of intense artistic relationships between the participating musicians.

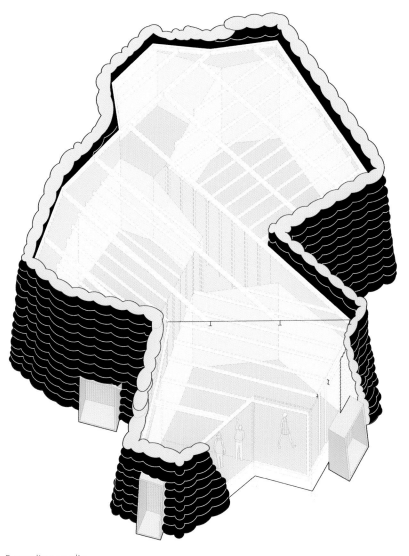

Recording studio

Ector Hoogstad Architects

IMd Engineering Office

Rotterdam, the Netherlands

Photographs: Petra Appelhof

The new premises of engineering consultancy firm IMd in Rotterdam are a far cry from run-of-the-mill working environments. A former steel plant has been transformed in an unorthodox manner into a "playground for engineers", in the words of architect Joost Ector of the Rotterdam firm Ector Hoogstad Architects.

Recycling is an important issue in the Netherlands today, due to a large amount of high-quality vacant building stock. The steel plant, on Rotterdam's Piekstraat, was not an obvious location for an office, but is uniquely placed with views over the river Maas.

Ector Hoogstad Architects (EHA) and IMd had already worked together on a large number of projects, and wished to collaborate again on this striking property that would inspire staff and help IMd position itself even more clearly as one of the leading design engineering firms in the Netherlands. Renovation of the existing shell of the building soon proved unrealistic, both technically and financially. In the end, all the work areas were created on two stories in air-conditioned zones against the closed end walls. From there, they look back into the hall, which houses pavilions with conference spaces, linked by footbridges and stairways. The hall itself has become a weakly air-conditioned cavity, ideal for informal consultations, lectures, exhibitions and lunches. Large new windows in what was originally a closed façade, in combination with the existing skylights in the roof, provide daylight and magnificent panoramas over the water.

While the layout is unusual for an office building it does have some distinct advantages. Users are continually in contact with the spatial and social heart of the organization, which stimulates encounter and involvement. The great hall also possesses optimum spatial tension: bridges, underpasses and stairs encourage movement and the potential to observe the people and spaces within it from ever-changing perspectives. Moreover, only air-conditioning the pavilions, rather than the whole hall, reduces energy consumption. The sustainability of the project is also assured by the use of light, recyclable materials and the use of the existing building as a base.

Everything that was already present in the building, such as the steel skeleton, the concrete floors and the masonry on the façade, was simply cleaned. New additions were made using a limited number of materials, which are new but very much in keeping with the industrial atmosphere; rough wood for stairs, clear glass and sheeting of translucent plastic. This sheeting gives the new walls a nice sense of diffusion, and even makes them slightly 'absent'. The consistent use of one color – bright yellow – unites the whole even more.

By reusing an existing building, the architects have not only created a project with a strong emphasis on sustainability and recycling, they have also created a dynamic work space full of tension – and harmony – between old and new.

Architecture:
Ector Hoogstad Architects
Client:
IMd Consulting Engineers
Project team (staff):
Joost Ector, Max Pape, Chris Arts, Markus Clarijs, ,Hetty Mommersteeg, Arja Hoogstad, Paul Sanders, Roel Wildervanck and Ridwan Tehupelasury
Contractor:
De Combi
Installation design and electrical installantions:
Unica
Structural advice:
IMd Consulting Engineers, Rotterdam
Building physics advice:
LBP Sight, Nieuwegein
Furniture design:
Ector Hoogstad Architects
Lighting:
Muuto, Philips and Lightyears via FormFocus
Walls and doors:
Qbic and Rodeca
Floors:
Bolon via Brandt bv, Oosterhout, Ege via Onstein Textiel Agenturen, Blaricum
Floor area:
2,000 sqm (21,500 sqft)

Site plan

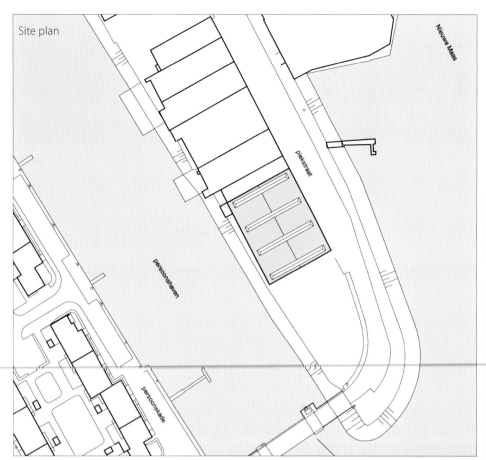

The aim was to built a striking property would not only inspire staff, but would also help IMd position itself even more clearly as one of the leading design engineering firms in the Netherlands.

42

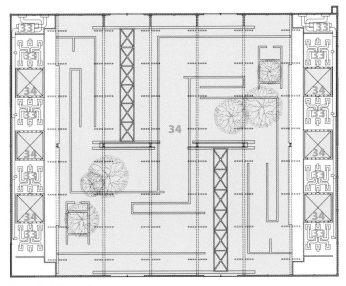

Technical floor plan

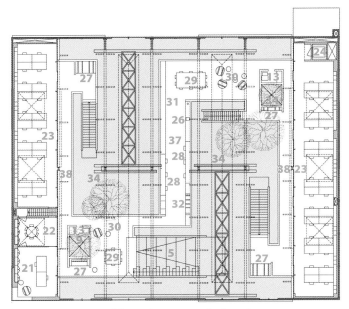

New situation second floor plan

0 2 5

north

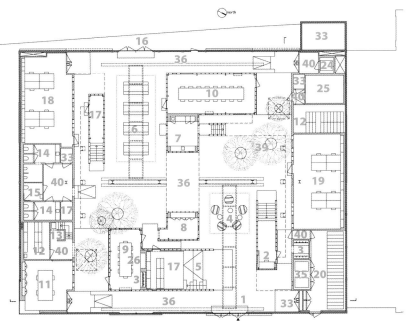

New situation ground floor plan

While the layout is unusual for an office building it does have some distinct advantages. Users are continually in contact with the spatial and social heart of the organization, which stimulates encounter and involvement. The consistent use of one color – bright yellow – unites the whole even more.

KEY

1. Entrance
2. Reception
3. Cloakroom
4. Waiting room
5. Stairs
6. Picnic tables
7. Kitchen
8. Photocopy room
9. Meeting room small
10. Meeting room large
11. Administration
12. Archives
13. Copy
14. Toilets
15. Disabled toilet
16. Terrace
17. Storage
18. Workspace
19. Multifunctional workspace
20. Bike park
21. Boardroom
22. Consulting room
23. Open workspace
24. Elevator
25. Server
26. Pantry
27. Meeting point
28. Individual workstation
29. Group workstation
30. Lounge
31. Library
32. Chaise longue
33. Technical space
34. Void
35. Container
36. Atrium
37. Bridge
38. Plateau
39. Trees
40. Anteroom

45

Longitudinal section

Cross section

0   2   5 m

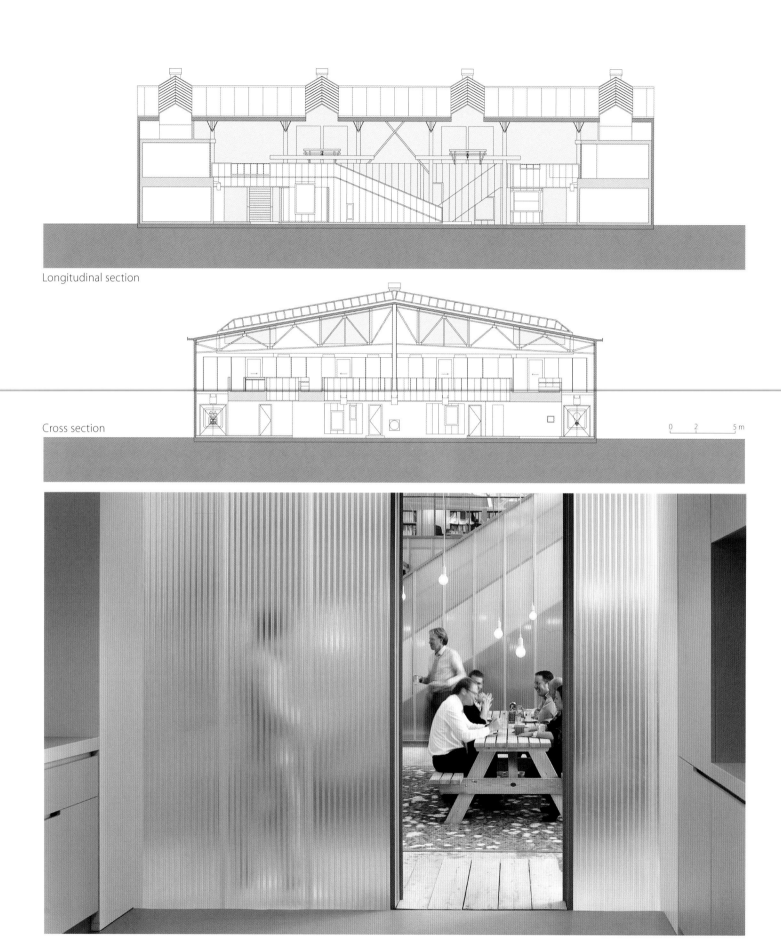

Edward Ogosta Architecture

Hybrid Office

Los Angeles, California, USA

Photographs: Edward Ogosta Architecture

Designed for a creative media agency of thirty workers, this office contains a menagerie of typological hybrids, which together engender a unique interior world. Existing somewhere between furniture and architecture, these hybrid objects infuse the office functions with new iconographic presence, and abstractly reference nature and the surrounding city. Collectively, they foster an atmosphere of creative intensity, and embody the idiosyncratic spirit of the company.

An existing 6,000 square foot tilt-up concrete warehouse provides a purified container into which the hybrids are deployed. Each hybrid synthesizes essential traits from two "parents" of differing typologies: for example, a set of bookshelves combined with the stepped form of an arena results in the book-arena, which functions both as storage and seating for office-wide meetings. Other hybrids include the tree-chair, mountain-offices, house-table, and cave-bed. Each is constructed from simple veneered plywood and white painted fiberboard (except for the house-table, which was custom built from manufactured office furniture). A variety of micro-scaled individual spaces and group-sized collective spaces are thus available to all workers.

The conceptual intertwining of the office interior and the exterior world expands the experiential possibilities of inhabitation. To sit in a chair as if inside a tree, or occupy a table as one would a house, is to prompt a rethinking of how we interact with objects and environments. Fundamental notions of dwelling and working are consequently upended, yet simultaneously clarified.

Architecture:
Edward Ogosta Architecture
Client:
Private Client
Area:
6,000 sqft (557 sqm)

Mountain

Offices

Mountain offices

+

=

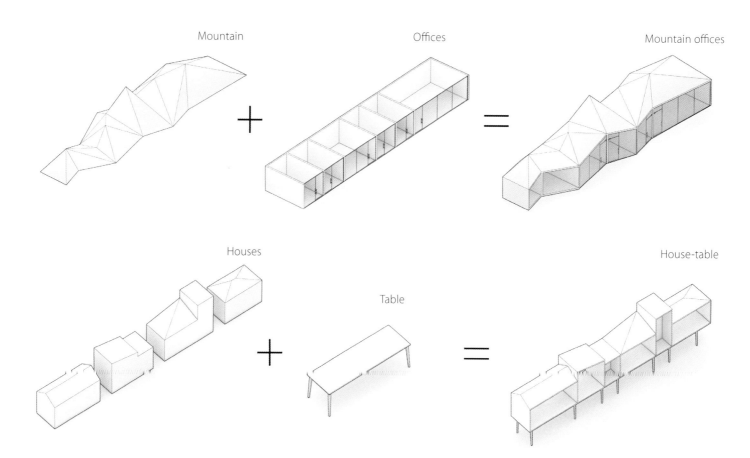

Houses

Table

House-table

+

=

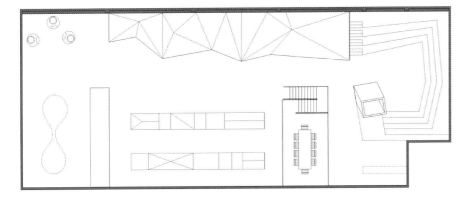

Mezzanine plan

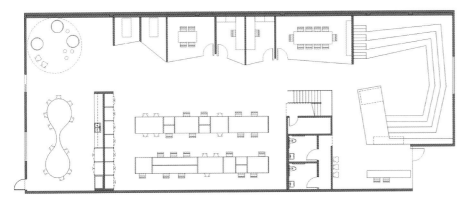

Ground floor plan

An existing 6,000 square foot concrete warehouse has been transformed with a series of hybrid inhabitable furniture elements into a workspace for a company of thirty people.

Bookshelves   Arena   Book arena

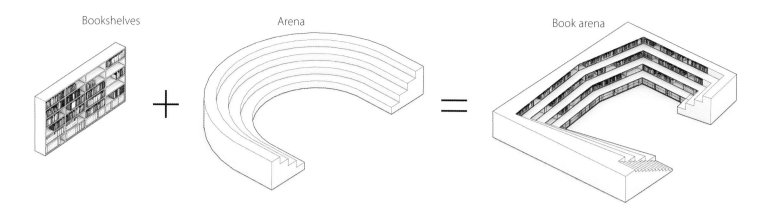

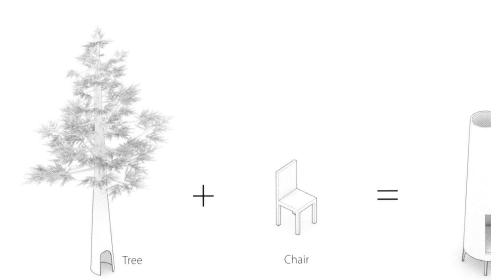

Tree + Chair = Tree-chair

Each hybrid synthesizes essential traits from two "parents" of differing typologies: for example, a set of bookshelves combined with the stepped form of an arena results in the book-arena, which functions both as storage and seating for office-wide meetings.

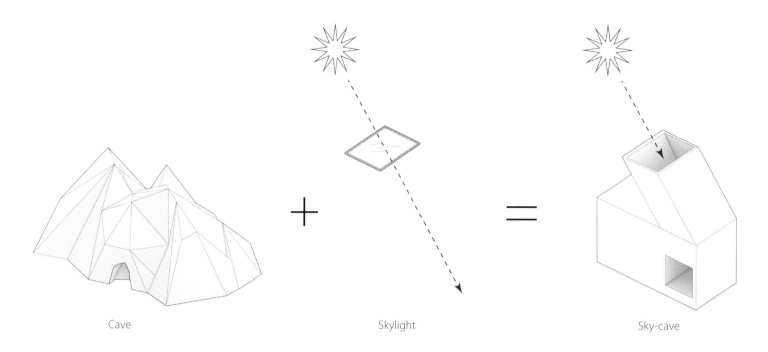

Cave   +   Skylight   =   Sky-cave

Supermachine Studio

Refurbishment of Saatchi & Saatchi Thailand offices

Bangkok, Thailand

Photographs: Wison Tungthunya

The renovation of the offices of Saatchi&Saatchi in Bangkok has resulted in an innovative and exciting workplace in which everyday objects become inspirational. The office is separated into two zones: the creative zone and the management zone. The former has been designed to be open and bright to foster open communication, the sharing of ideas and mutual inspiration – enabling the creative team to work as a family. On the other side of the office, the management zone has a more sober atmosphere that is punctuated with colorful decorations as a reminder that they too can have fun at work. The center of the plan is occupied by a playful trophy wall, a bicycle wall for staff and visitors' bikes and a facilities zone with bright pink walls.

Each component of the interior has been designed to serve the requirements of the office while making everyday tasks that bit more fun. Expanding the functionality of everyday objects has led to creations such as the bicycle meeting table that separates into two smaller tables – it is at once more fun and more versatile than a normal table. Another item is the counter on wheels located in the lobby: a stylized representation of a bus, it serves both as the reception desk and as a mobile café/bar counter. There are also meeting pods inspired in sections of train carriages. The pods offer a level of privacy and the sense of entering a different space. Another social gathering space is the bar that extends into a daybed. It can be used as a mini kitchen/bar with space for a fridge and glasses or as a reading/resting unit with the storage space occupied by books.

Arquitecture:

Supermachine Studio: Pitupong Chaowakul, Suchart Ouypornchaisakul, Peechaya Mekasuvanroj, Santi Sarasuphab

Constructor:

St.Classic Co., Ltd.

Client:

Joel Clement/Saatchi & Saatchi Thailand

Area:

400 sqm (4,290 sqft)

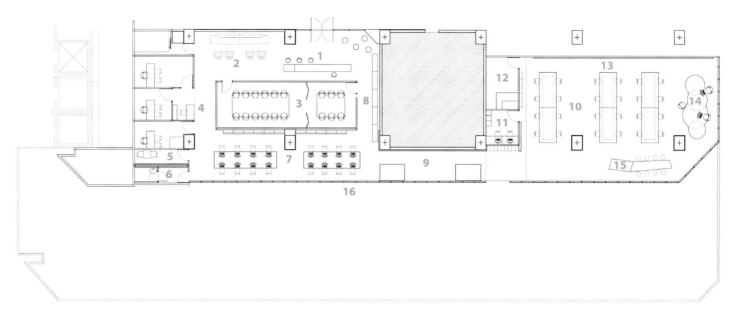

GROUND FLOOR PLAN

1. Reception bus	5. Pantry	9. Meeting pod area	13. Monster wall
2. Waiting area	6. Toilet	10. Creative department	14. Creative director table
3. Meeting room	7. Admin. department	11. Editing room	15. Mini bar
4. Managing director department	8. Trophy table	12. Photocopy room	16. Outdoor terrace

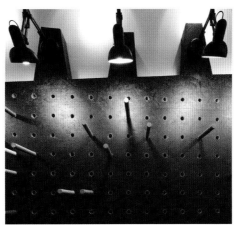

A monster message board covers the entire length of the wall in the creative zone. Staff can interact with different parts of the animal, which are variously furnished with holes, pins, lighting, and shelving.

The design for the refurbishment of the Saatchi&Saatchi offices in Bangkok focuses on transforming familiar items into innovative yet functional elements for everyday use. Since space is limited, each element serves multiple functions while at the same time contributing to creating an inspiring working environment.

Shimoda Design Group with Steelcase Inc.

Steelcase Work Café

Grand Rapids, Michigan, USA

Photographs: contributed by the architects

The Work Café project was inspired by three specific ideas, the first being to refresh the global head-quarters of the company in time for their 100th anniversary. A 1983 cafeteria was refurbished, and three large training rooms were converted into a new Work Café of approximately 23,000 sqft (2,100 sqm). The first challenge of the project was to connect the Work Café with the rest of the building. We accomplished this by creating a grand stair with a custom designed fiberglass stent. This gesture was a symbolic first step in connecting the past with the future.

Another aim was to integrate food and work through a palette of place and a palette of posture. Work-spaces are integrated around the social aspects of food. There are a variety of seating arrangements (lounge to dining) combined with degrees of spatial intimacy. These elements revolve around two food centers: a cafeteria and a nourishment beverage bar. This idea of nourishment was expanded, and the space also seeks to nourish the connection between local and global. The main cafeteria is designed to take advantage of the local bounty of West Michigan, but is seasoned with the tastes of a global company. Complementing the main cafeteria is the nourishment bar, dedicated to high quality coffee and tea. The nourishment bar is coupled with an electronic global wall and becomes a real time connection for all the employees to participate in.

Architecture:
Shimoda Design Group with Steelcase Inc.

Project team:
Joey Shimoda AIA, Principal;
James Ludwig, Vice President of Global Design (Steelcase Inc.);
Cherie Johnson, Design Manager (Steelcase Inc.);
Susan Chang, Project Architect;
Dan Allen; Todd Tuntland; David Khuong;
Benjamin Grobe; Ying-Ling Sun;
Andre Krause; Elizabeth Cao

Structural Engineer:
Robert Darvas Associates, P.C.

Mechanical, Electrical and Landscape:
Progressive AE

Area:
23,000 sqft (2,100 sqm)

A 1983 cafeteria was refurbished, and three large training rooms were converted into a new Work Café

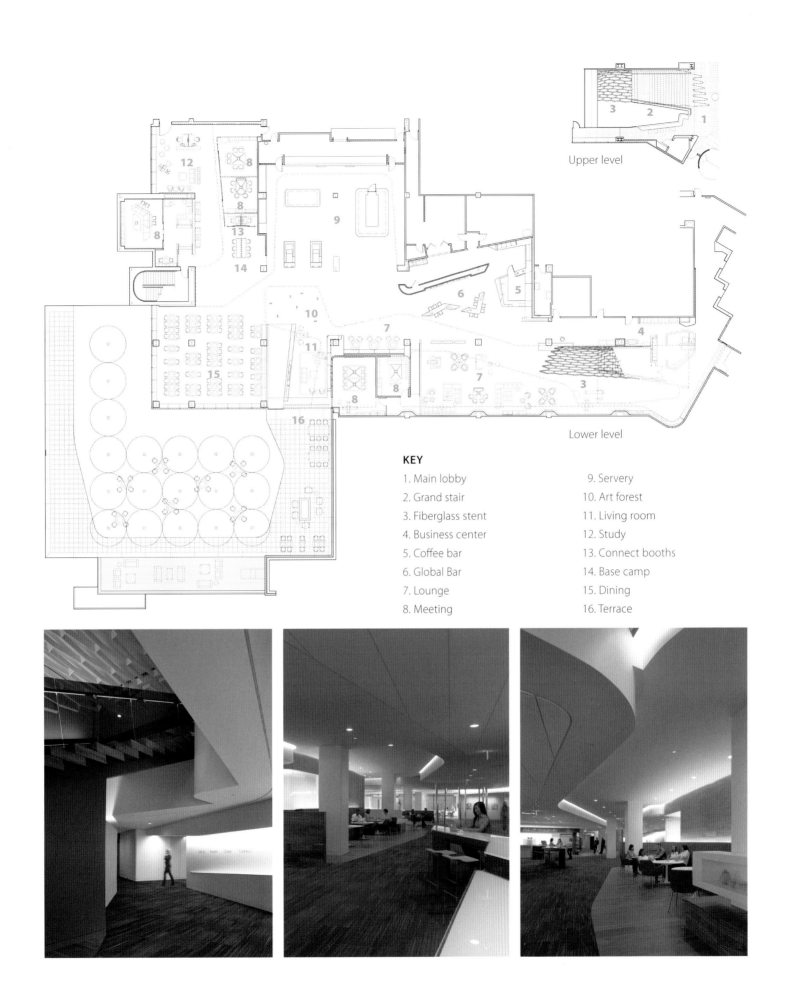

Upper level

Lower level

KEY

1. Main lobby
2. Grand stair
3. Fiberglass stent
4. Business center
5. Coffee bar
6. Global Bar
7. Lounge
8. Meeting

9. Servery
10. Art forest
11. Living room
12. Study
13. Connect booths
14. Base camp
15. Dining
16. Terrace

Workspaces are integrated around the social aspects of food. There are a variety of seating arrangements (lounge to dining) combined with degrees of spatial intimacy. These elements revolve around two food centers: a cafeteria and a nourishment beverage bar.

Pedra Silva Architects

Fraunhofer Portugal

Oporto, Portugal

Photographs: João Morgado

Fraunhofer Portugal is a non-profit private research association forming part of the German Fraunhofer-Gesellschaft, the largest organization for applied research in Europe. Although not well known among the general public, Fraunhofer is responsible for many important innovations, such as the MP3 file format, and many advances in workplace organization research.

Pedra Silva Architects were selected in an open competition to design the new Oporto headquarters for the research body, to be located at the Oporto University Technology and Science Park. Their design conveys Fraunhofer's innovative philosophy, at once simple, positive and dynamic. The innovative workplace layout and organizational elements from Fraunhofer Office Innovation Center in Stuttgart (Germany) were also an important input to the project, adding another layer to the architects' concept. The 1,660 square meters of research facilities occupy two floors in a new building. The circulation strategy forms the backbone of the project: the spaces are distributed along a walkway that follows the glazed façade. The workspaces are generated by an undulating plane that winds through the open-plan floors to create spaces of different sizes and characters. The visually dynamic spaces that result from this gesture are reinforced by the clear use of color. The sinuous surface becomes in turn ceiling, wall or the floor of offices and meeting rooms, guaranteeing visual continuity, movement and flow through the length of the interior.

Another important feature of the design is the introduction of small social and meeting spaces, referred to as "silent rooms", which provide the opportunity for personal retreat, as well as informal meetings and rest breaks. These spaces are intended to generate a creative environment and promote comfort and wellbeing among the researchers.

Architecture:
Pedra Silva Architects
Project coordination:
Luis Pedra Silva with ENGEXPOR
Design team:
Hugo Ramos, Rita Pais, Jette Fyhn, Dina Castro, André Góis Fernandes, Ricardo Sousa, Bruno Almeida
Graphic design:
Rita and Joana Coimbra
MEP design:
JCT with GATENGEL
Lighting:
Astratec with Prolicht Lighting
Workplace Furniture:
BENE
Social furniture:
Empatias
Contractor:
BEC – Braga Equipamento e Construção
Project area:
1,660 sqm (17,800 sqft)

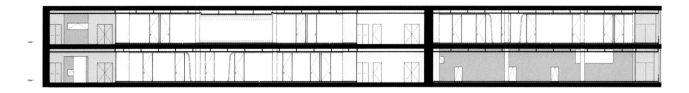

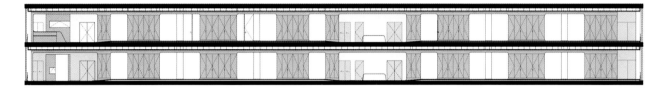

Sections

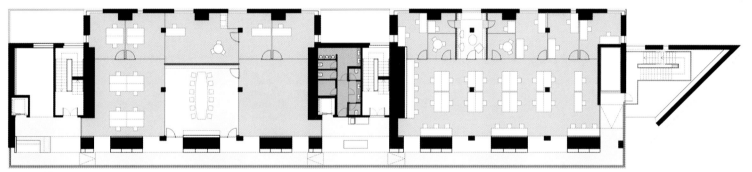

Second floor

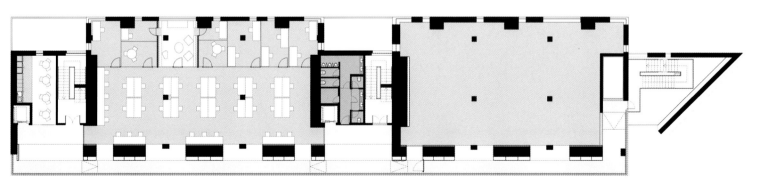

First floor

79

Pedra Silva Architects were selected to design the new Oporto headquarters for Fraunhofer Portugal, at the Oporto University Technology and Science Park. Their design conveys Fraunhofer's innovative philosophy: at once simple, positive and dynamic.

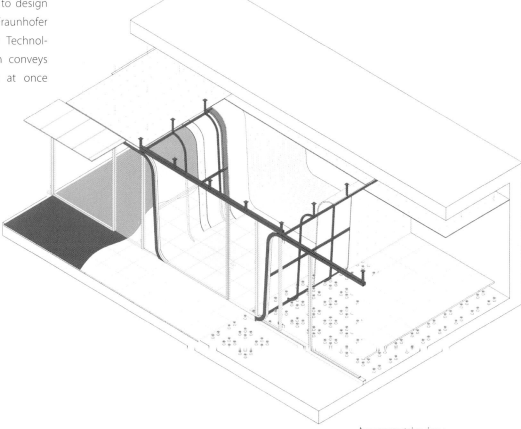

Axonometric view

The 1,660 square meters of research facilities occupy two floors in a new building. The circulation strategy forms the backbone of the project: the spaces are distributed along a walkway that follows the glazed façade.

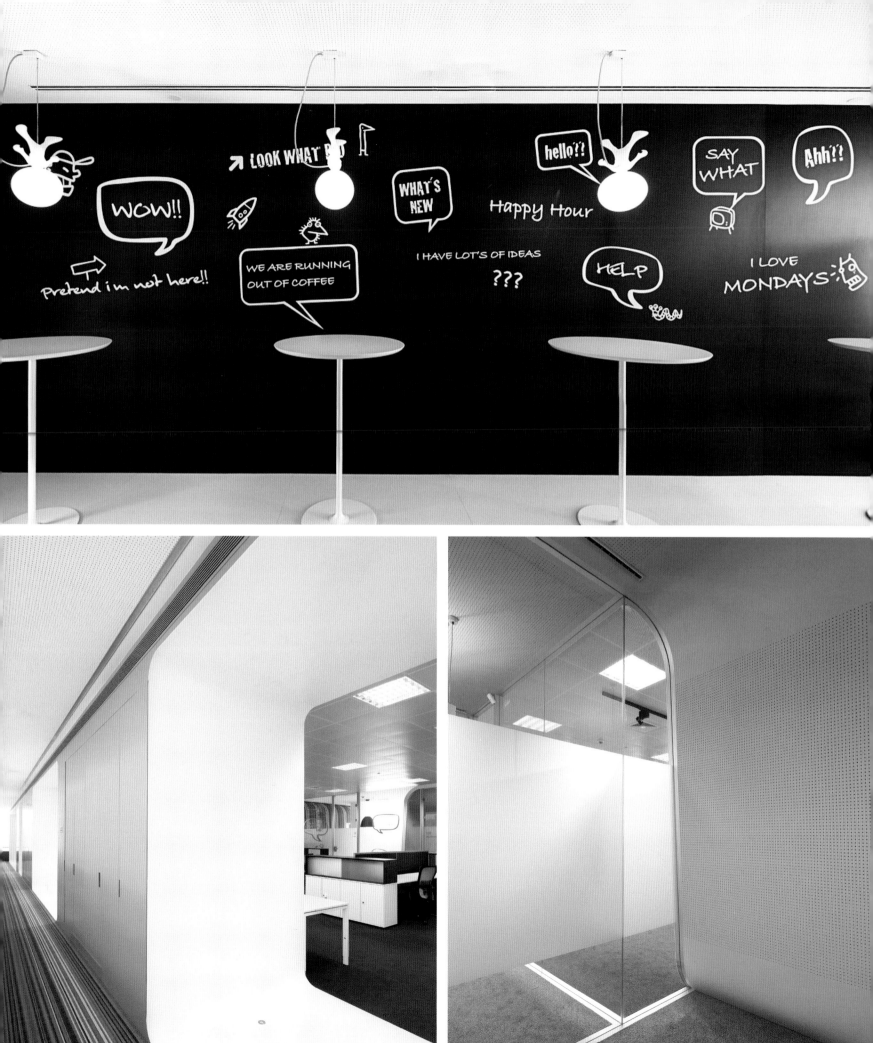

The workspaces are generated by an undulating plane that winds through the open-plan floors to create spaces of different sizes and characters. The sinuous surface becomes in turn ceiling, wall or the floor of offices and meeting rooms, guaranteeing visual continuity, movement and flow through the length of the interior.

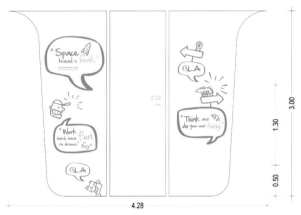

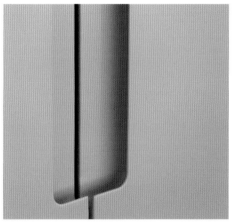

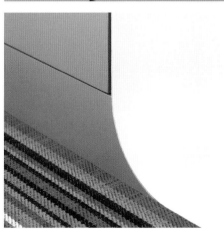

WINDOW DETAIL

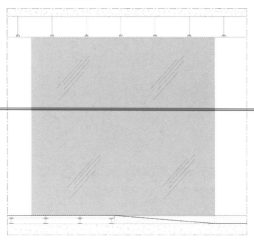

Elevation

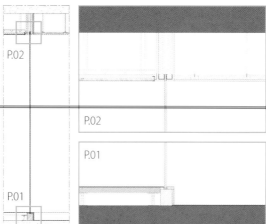

P.02

P.02

P.01

P.01

Cut

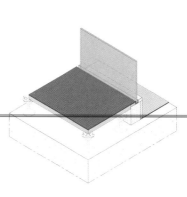

Isometric view of pavement brackets

Floor plan

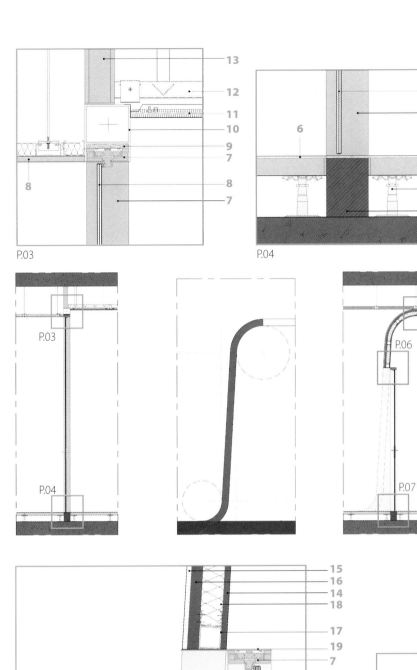

P.03

P.04

P.03

P.04

P.05

P.06

P.07

KEY

1. Existing slab

2. Brick wall as acoustic barrier

3. Pavement bracket

4. Raised pavement in standard modules of
   600 x 600 mm

5. Carpet

6. Carpet

7. "ECOWALL" partitions

8. Colorless tempered glass door

9. Acoustic insulation, 10 mm

10. Structure made of 4 mm metal profiles

11. Perforated false roof, painted white

12. False roof suspension structure

13. Structure composed of tubular metal profiles
    fixed to existing slab

14. Perforated plasterboard

15. Vinyl siding

16. 26 mm medium density fiberboard

17. Structure composed of square-section tubular
    metal profiles

18. Rockwool acoustic insulation

19. Metal sheet, 3 mm

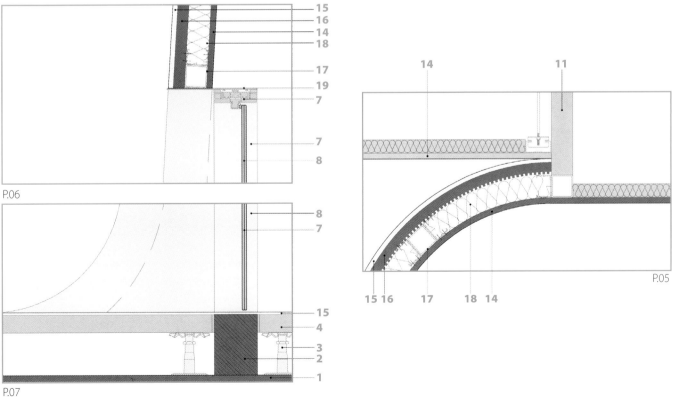

P.06

P.07

P.05

87

Pinkeye Crossover Design Studio

Pinkeye Crossover Offices

Antwerp, Belgium   **Photographs:** Frederik Vercruysse

When the office space adjacent to Pinkeye's headquarters became available, the crossover design studio jumped at the opportunity to expand their workspace. Their former office had become too cramped and didn't match the needs of its varied workforce. The company is a multidisciplinary design studio, with various in-house specializations – product developers, graphic designers, interior architects, marketers; in short, a dynamic firm with a highly diverse output. This called for a communal area that would facilitate interaction to a certain extent, with smaller workstations to group together and brainstorm about a certain project. The central element in the design of the 600 sqm (6,500 sqft) space is a dividing wall that runs the length of the workspace. Clad in diagonally framed wooden beams, the wall's interplay of lines creates structure and atmosphere, providing a framework that accommodates several more intimate spaces.

Half moon shaped cut outs create windows that reveal more intimate rooms, an intervention to create quiet, private workspaces in the overall open office design. An elongated office table houses 18 monitors, mice, graphic pads and keyboards for as many creative heads.

The interior is a mixture of design and practicality. The pinewood struts that support the wall are intentionally left raw and the four perfectly curved openings in the tall wall are placed symmetrically, which gives the entire space a 'sacred' feel, although in fact it is a childhood filled with building treehouses that lies at the root of the design. Black and white hanging lights hover above the central work table like UFOs. At one end of the room two spaces are set behind glass doors: a rather sober conference room and a more decorative creativity room. There is vintage furniture, and petrol-blue curtains can be used to hide away the whiteboard walls, a smart invention to keep discussions with clients out of sight where necessary. A beamer allows employees to write on the wall via the projector.

Parallel to the work island, the smaller units house a room for conference calls, a meeting room and a library. The spacious lunch area, a space that could equally serve as a bar, is set to the rear. The bar itself is clad in gold, with diamond- shaped cut-outs outlined in black, and is aimed at encouraging staff to sit and eat together. Opposite the bar are several smaller tables with Emeco Navy chairs.

Exiting the offices, a text in one of the windows of the smaller workspaces, sculpted in matte black metal, reads 'You Work Harder'. A message so direct has to conjure up a smile. Mission Accomplished!

Architecture:
Pinkeye Crossover Design Studio
Area:
600 sqm (6,500 sqft)

Pinkeye's ambitious new office reflects the attitude and work approach of the growing cross-over design studio – and it looks good, too.

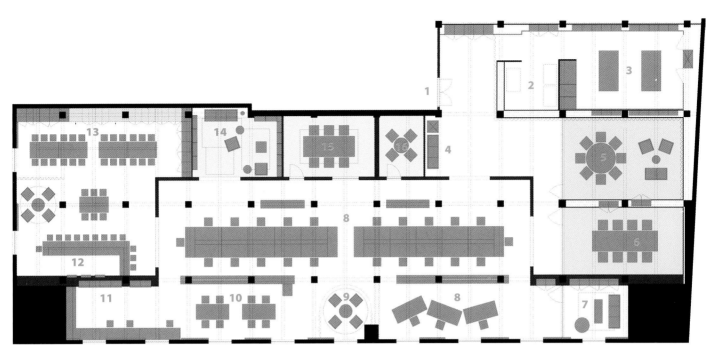

FLOOR PLAN

1. Entrance
2. Storage
3. Atelier
4. Waiting room

5. Brainstorm room
6. Large meeting room
7. Salon
8. Bureau

9. Booth
10. Project tables
11. Material library
12. Bar

13. Kitchen
14. Library
15. Small meeting room
16. Conf. call room

Exiting the offices, a text in one of the windows of the smaller workspaces, sculpted in matte black metal, reads 'You Work Harder'. A message so direct has to conjure up a smile.

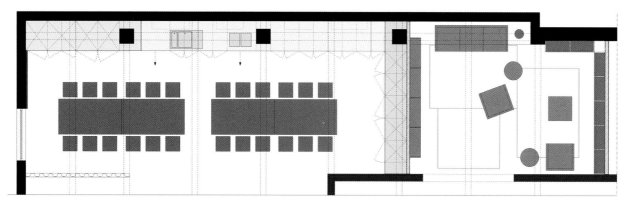

Kitchen and library ground floor

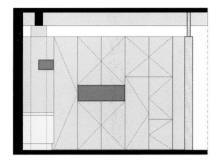

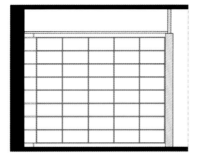

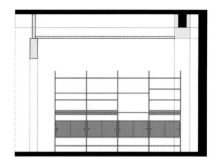

Kitchen view   Library view   Library view

OpenAD

McCann- Erickson Riga & McCann- Erickson Riga PR

Riga, Latvia

Photographs: Maris Lagzdins, Didzis Grodze

The McCann Erickson Riga offices and McCann Erickson Riga PR offices are located on different floors of the same building, and share a common theme which identifies them as being from the same company.

In the McCann Erickson Riga offices, functional planning is a stylized union between inner rooms and a conceptualized exterior - "streets" have been formed, separated into "blocks," that contain "houses" with windows, façades, podiums and recessed flower beds in the floor. They have been finished and furnished using simple materials, lacquered MDF boards and white paint. The interiors are largely finished with recycled materials and leftover pieces of timber. Lamps are made of wide plasterboard tubes, which were previously used as fabric roles. This is a low-budget project, which uses simple materials to play on the popular "trash style" of interior decoration.

The McCann-Erickson Riga PR office is a conceptual continuation for the McCann-Erickson Riga office, which had already been built and is located in the same building. The idea of the stylization of exterior space indoors is continued, with a "courtyard" being the central workplace area, and a separated block which comprises a "house" with windows and façades. The house contains a meeting room and a studio/media training room. The linear composition of the space is demarcated and followed by the overhead lighting. The building is inhabited on all sides, and there is an integrated windowsill for reading magazines or perching and brainstorming.

The furnishings and finishings are simple here as in the company´s sister office. Materials include lacquered MDF boards, grey lacquered blastula, a straw colored carpet and imitation grass that creates a symbolic stylization of a courtyard and meadow.

Architecture:
OPEN ARCHITECTURE AND DESIGN
Zane Tetere, Rita Saldeniece
Client:
McCann Erickson-Riga
Area:
125 sqm (1,300 sqft)

McCann- Erickson Riga

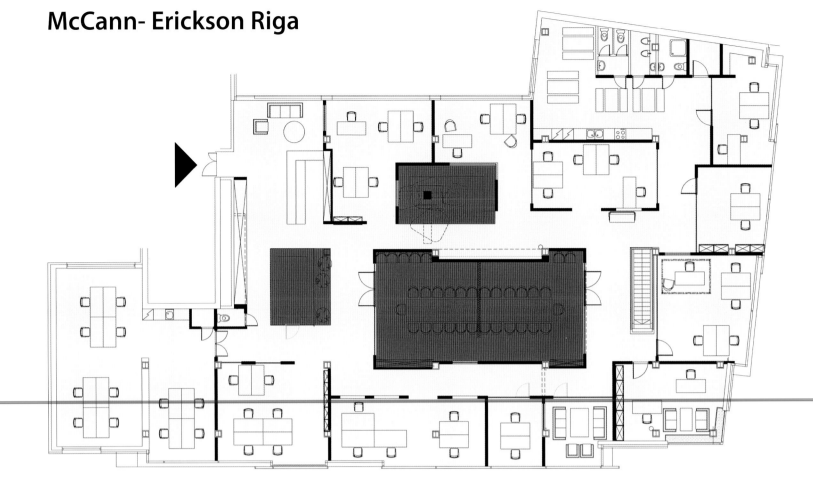

Ground floor plan

In an area a little removed from the main action of the patio is an elevated 'library tree,' with the books hanging from its trunk and branches. With this special touch, the employees can consult the books they need lying on the lawn, or on the comfortable benches nearby.

McCann- Erickson Riga PR

The linear composition also translates to the lighting, which comes from above. Underneath, the different working spaces and the 'building' are organized, with access from all sides to improve functionality.

The distribution of the offices is completely functional and is organized so as to unify the interior rooms and create an exterior 'patio,' which contains the different individual workspaces.

Garcia Tamjidi Architecture Design

Index Ventures

San Francisco, California, USA

Photographs: Joe Fletcher Photography

Already established in European markets with offices in London and Geneva, this third base was designed in California for highly creative, collaborative venture capital team Index Ventures. The new offices are located on the top floor of a historic brick and timber building in SOMA with views to AT&T Park. A truncated light well was designed around an existing skylight to maximize daylight, flooding the rooms with bright white light. The walls are white too, but the expansive and clean brightness is tempered somewhat by exposed brick walls and timber beams, recalling the buildings past and seamlessly melding the past and future of the city.

The design also insists on practicality, and provides for staff with busy and active lifestyles. A café, bathrooms and showers have been incorporated, so that team members can arrive from abroad or by bicycle and hit the ground running.

Smart technology has also been utilized: the latest in 'smart' lighting by Redwood Systems, an Index Venture partner, runs on low voltage and adapts real-time by tracking room-by-room use and natural day-lighting during the course of the year. Overall, the emphasis is on intelligent design, functional space and ecological sustainability, while at the same time provided staff in the San Francisco offices with a pleasant and stimulating working environment.

Architecture:
Garcia Tamjidi Architecture Designi
Builder:
Fisher Development Inc.

A truncated light well was designed around an existing skylight to maximize daylight, flooding the rooms with bright white light. The walls are white too, but the expansive and clean brightness is tempered somewhat by exposed brick walls and timber beams, recalling the buildings past and seamlessly melding the past and future of the city.

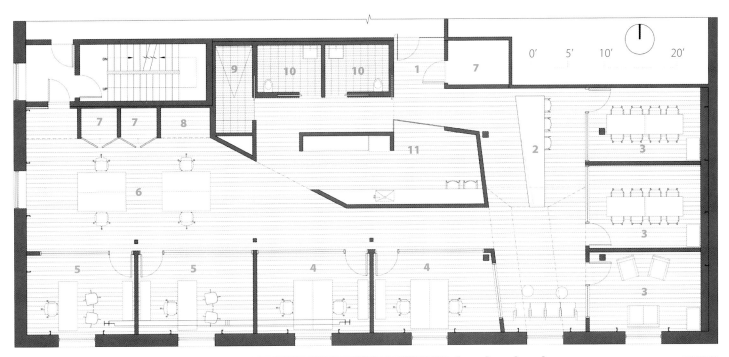

FLOOR PLAN

1. Entry
2. Reception
3. Meeting room
4. Double office
5. Private office
6. Open office
7. Storage
8. Copy print
9. Shower
10. Bathroom
11. Cafe

Smart technology has been utilized: the latest in 'smart' lighting by Redwood Systems, an Index Venture partner, runs on low voltage and adapts real-time by tracking room-by-room use and natural day-lighting during the course of the year.

V Arc

iSelect Offices

Cheltenham, Victoria, Australia

Photographs: contributed by V Arc

Australian interior design and architectural company V Arc were charged with designing a new office space of health insurance providers iSelect and delivered an unconventional, but striking and appropriate result. The 4,800 sqm (51,700 sqft) site, split across three levels, marries contemporary design practices and space planning with clear design drivers: design an environment that is fun, quirky and gives back to the staff, and create an environment that is professional yet entertaining – promoting social interaction throughout.

The Front of House makes use of the iSelect corporate colours, orange and white. With stark white epoxy floors and bold splashes of orange, the front of house has a number of quirky spaces including the round "interrogation room" and white internal stair which was part of the design brief to ensure great vertical integration throughout the floors.

Throughout the call center and corporate workplace, the design incorporates a variety of meeting, touchdown and informal collaboration points for team discussions and a two-lane running track around the core to facilitate walking meetings. Just one of many design quirks, the running track leads to a soccer pitch, sun hammocks complete with ocean views, whippet stool and a slide which exits the façade of the building and lands you in a ball pit within their full service 300sqm cafe and entertainment precinct which sits adjacent to the reception and front of house meeting suites.

Around the floors are meeting pods of all shapes and sizes, including sleep pods, a nursing room, an authentic 1940's phone booth (quiet room), massage pods and various herds of sculpted ponies throughout the space.

The café is a revolutionary departure from a typical workspace, and is intended as a heart of the office. An outdoor area contains everything from shade sails to a commercial BBQ for the warmer months and a full service cafe with external provider to cater for breakfasts, lunches, Friday night gatherings and functions.

A major goal in the design was to provide adequate working space for optimum comfort. In the finished office, unobstructed circulation networks allow for communication and contact between staff. Previously, the central elevator was the primary means of navigating the site. Key objectives included the increased interaction between staff departments, which led to the implementation of a central interconnecting stair and slide to promote vertical circulation.

Architecture:
V Arc
Client:
iSelect
Area:
4,800 sqm (51,700 sqft)

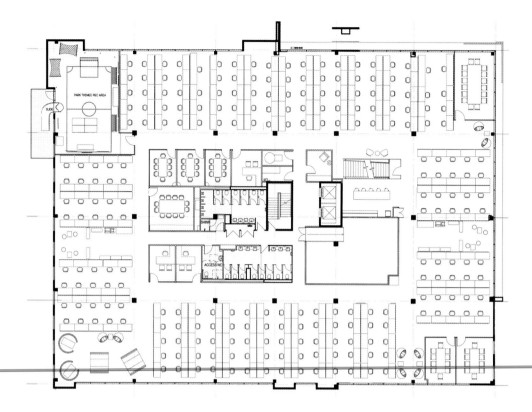

First floor plan

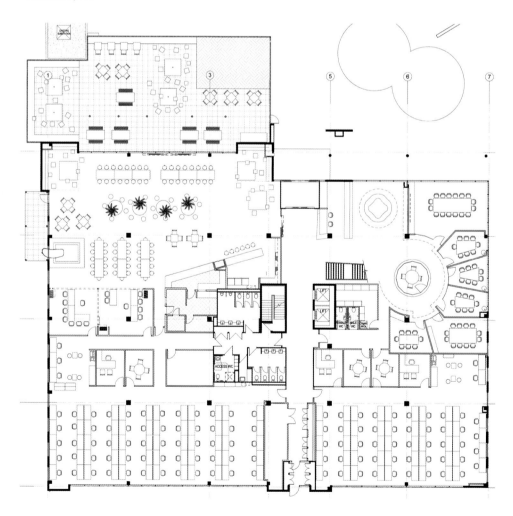

Ground floor plan

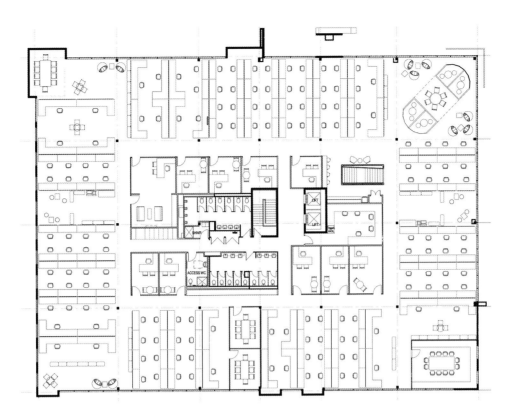

Second floor plan

With stark white epoxy floors and bold splashes of orange, the front of house has a number of quirky spaces including the round "interrogation room" and white internal stair which was part of the design brief to ensure great vertical integration throughout the floors.

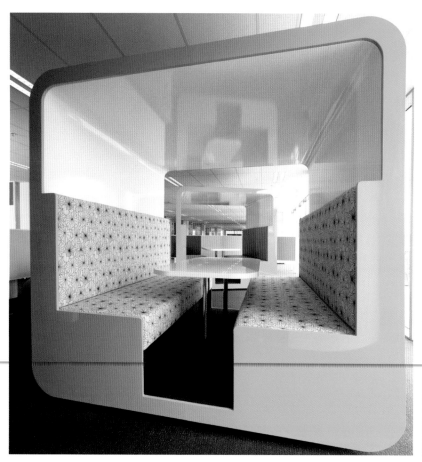

Around the floors are meeting pods of all shapes and sizes, including sleep pods, a nursing room, an authentic 1940's phone booth (quiet room), massage pods and various herds of sculpted ponies throughout the space.

PENSON

YouTube Space

London, UK   **Photographs:** contributed by PENSON

Completed in 2012, YouTube's new offices in the heart of Covent Garden, London, are already turning heads in style and design circles. The space features Del Boy's (of much-loved British Sitcom Only Fools and Horses) living room in Mandela House, Peckham, a cinema sealed off by the PENSON trademark Air-Lock doors; sound proof recording studios, squishy sunken snugs and environmentally-friendly back-of-stage walls. These have been made from quickly erected timber, much like stage sets. There are also ergonomic video conferencing rooms, meeting booths and film viewing pods. All the different aspects of the design contribute to a highly functional yet unique space. It is both stimulating to new ideas and calming to offering a focused creative atmosphere. The desk areas are oases of calm, with views of London's skyline.

At the core of the space is a YouTube walk of fame, with padded walls and a long sumptuous couch that reflect a modern twist on old English cinemas. The Creator Space has been designed in collaboration with YouTube, CBT and DreamTek and includes a Green Room, editing suites and two large acoustic filming spaces. A silver and glittering reception area dazzles external visitors, YouTubers and the odd passing celebrity. Silver fabric walls form Flight Pods, another PENSON trademark, which provide secluded meeting spaces for comfortable, creative collaboration. There are integrated whiteboards built into them for spontaneous brainstorming sessions. The space provides desks and a variety of cubby holes for collaborative group work. A vivid yellow micro-kitchen is featured in celebration of the famous Only Fools and Horses episode "Yellow Peril", in which Del Boy wheels a deal to redecorate his local Chinese take-away in faulty luminous yellow paint.

Lee Penson, the founder of PENSON says that "with Del's famous cocktail bar, complete with shaker, glass and umbrella, it's great fun to work at YouTube London. Del's twin porcelain dogs, 60s bamboo-shoot wallpaper and Granddad's awful choice of curtains and carpet, chintz drinks trolley and life ring, creates just the right level of loveable-rogue taste. The Brits love Del, and YouTuber's love this HQ".

The space is ecologically friendly, since many materials have high recycled content, are fully recycled, reclaimed, water-based or fully natural. The project is only a few points short of LEED Platinum, which is a huge achievement for an interior redesign.

Architecture:
PENSON

Client:
YouTube

Contractor:
Parkeray

Project Managers:
CBRE

Studio Design:
Dreamtek

Desks:
Bene

Lighting:
Zero supplied by Inform,
Diesel lights supplied by Atrium

Flooring:
Object Carpets, supplied by Chroma.
Nora flooring

Furniture:
Moroso, Dead good Supplied by Day 2

Finishes/Fabrics:
Kvadrat fabrics

Joinery:
ADS Joinery

Graphics:
Castleton's signs

The space features Del Boy´s (of much-loved British Sitcom Only Fools and Horses) living room in Mandela House, Peckham, a cinema sealed off by the PENSON trademark Air-Lock doors; sound proof recording studios, squishy sunken snugs and environmentally-friendly back-of-stage walls.

The space is ecologically friendly, since many materials have high recycled content, are fully recycled, reclaimed, water-based or fully natural. The project is only a few points short of LEED Platinum, which is a huge achievement for an interior redesign.

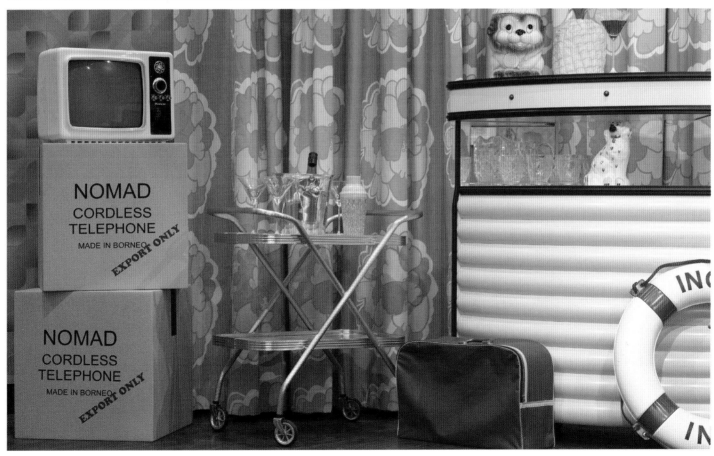

Silver fabric walls form Flight Pods, another PEN-SON trademark, which provide secluded meeting spaces for comfortable, creative collaboration. There are integrated whiteboards built into them for spontaneous brainstorming sessions.

PULL

DO NOT
TURN TO OPEN

Friit 1

Friit 2

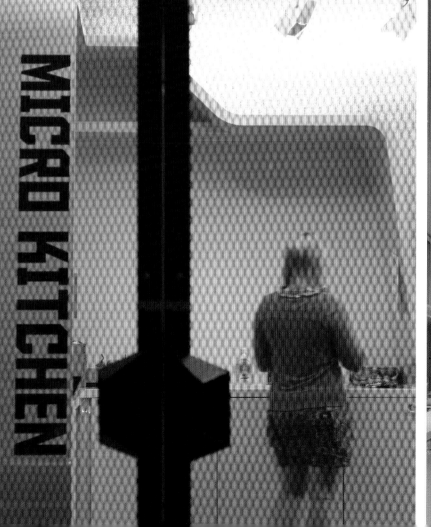

MICRO KITCHEN

M Moser Associates

Fair day's work: Ogilvy & Mather Guangzhou

Guangzhou, China

Photographs: contributed by Virgile Bertrand

A need for a larger space to accommodate a growing staff was only half the story behind Ogilvy & Mather Guangzhou's move from a prime CBD office to premises in a new urban 'arts and culture' zone on the city's fringe. As well as providing room to expand, the global communications firm envisioned its new Guangzhou outpost as a 'carnival of ideas' that would act as a lightning rod for new talent in spite of a relatively remote location.

The new workplace would occupy the ground and first floors of an industrial-style building nestled among the galleries and cafes of Fang Cun district. Including a large mezzanine later interposed between the floor plates, the volume offered a total are of 886 sqm (9,500 sqft). From this starting point, the M Moser team began organizing the space to reflect the client's operational and technological needs.

The organization of the space is a reflection of how Ogilvy works, with emphasis on collaboration and creativity. This results in a mostly 'public' ground floor, with a reception area that flows into a pantry and projection room. Marketing staff have a separate work area nearby. There is also a mezzanine that is more 'private,' with a marketing room and think tank. The upper floor is mainly open-plan workspace.

The 'Carnival of ideas' theme was finally engaged in literally, with a space full of playful details, such as a bright red staircase that evokes a cinema marquee. It functions as a 'red corridor', drawing people through the office, and also defines the transition between client/break-out spaces at the front and the offices at the rear.

Exuberant details take users of the building on a journey of discovery... such as a boardroom featuring ornate wall panels and a carousel horse which functions as an overhead projector. Although many features look to be vintage, they were actually custom-made for the offices.

A concealed door opens to a spacious break-out/pantry area whose similarly exuberant carnival theme is balanced with solidly multipurpose layout.

The loft/mezzanine, which can be incorporated due to the building's generous ceiling height and is accessed via a suspended walkway leading off the staircase, is ideal for brainstorming sessions. It also provides a perch from which to observe the activity unfolding below.

The ultimate destination of the 'red corridor' is the upper floor workspace. Here, the surreal funfair atmosphere gives way to a quiet flood of natural light and a flowing open-plan work space. A prominent feature wall invites staff to share and shape their ideas. Balconies arranged around the volume offer access to fresh air and views of the surrounding neighborhood. A final burst of funfair style emerges in the break-out area, where a brutal industrial-style concrete ceiling and plain brick walls contrast with clubby leather armchairs and a miniature carousel complete with horses.

Architecture:
M Moser Associates
Client:
Ogilvy &Mather
Area:
886 sqm (9,500 sqft)

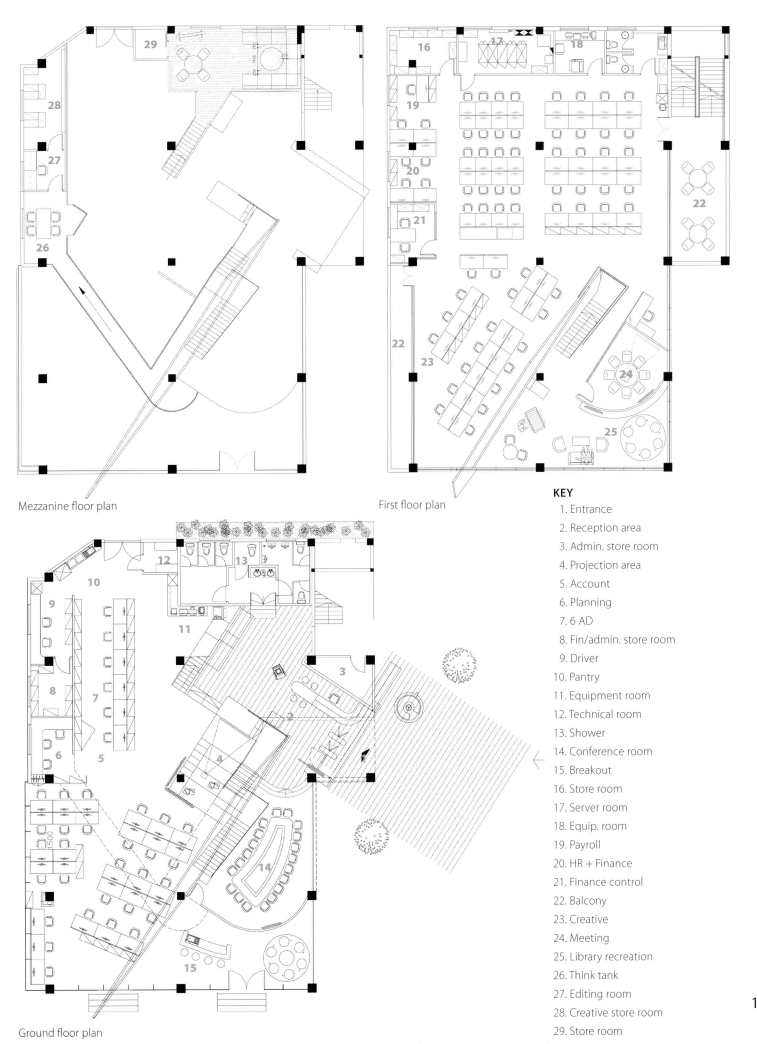

Mezzanine floor plan

First floor plan

Ground floor plan

KEY

1. Entrance
2. Reception area
3. Admin. store room
4. Projection area
5. Account
6. Planning
7. 6 AD
8. Fin/admin. store room
9. Driver
10. Pantry
11. Equipment room
12. Technical room
13. Shower
14. Conference room
15. Breakout
16. Store room
17. Server room
18. Equip. room
19. Payroll
20. HR + Finance
21. Finance control
22. Balcony
23. Creative
24. Meeting
25. Library recreation
26. Think tank
27. Editing room
28. Creative store room
29. Store room

135

Exuberant details take users of the building on a journey of discovery... such as a boardroom featuring ornate wall panels and a carousel horse which functions as an overhead projector. The ultimate destination of the 'red corridor' is the upper floor workspace. Here, the surreal funfair atmosphere gives way to a quiet flood of natural light and a flowing open-plan work space.

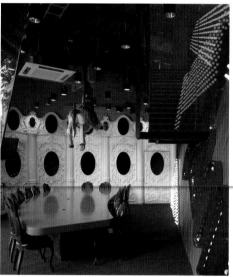

Dirk van Berkel

Univar Europe Antwerp

Antwerp, Belgium

Photographs: Frans Strous

In their search for office space where board members could meet and consult with their colleagues, Univar Europe found a former warehouse in the harbor area of Antwerp. Both inside and outside of the warehouse were considered heritage, and the building's listed status imposed a number of limitations on the project to transform the warehouse into new office space. One such restriction was that nothing could be attached to the beams, ceilings and floors. To overcome this, a 'floating' computer system floor was installed, which allows for cables to be wired for each workspace.

The meeting rooms and conference room are made of a sectional metal structures, which are rigid enough to allow the rooms to be freestanding in the space, without requiring them to be attached to the ceiling or columns. General lighting was provided by means of a rail with attached spotlights. This rail system is placed above the metal beams without attachments. The spotlights can be fixed anywhere on the rail, and provide sufficient lighting to use the space as an office. Individual lamps have also been integrated into the desks for extra light. Meanwhile, the combination of overhead and desk lighting creates a cozier, homelike atmosphere in which to work.

Daylight only enters the warehouse windows at the front and back and the depth of each floor is 30 meters. It was therefore decided to place all elements freely in the space and to use glass walls for the meeting and conference rooms so as to allow as much daylight as possible into all workspaces, and to avoid the 'locked-in' feeling of some offices. The conference room is fitted with net curtains for more privacy if required. These curtains also aid in noise absorption.

In the left-hand corner at the back of the building is a lunch area with a kitchenette and some tables where the co-workers can have a cup of coffee or some lunch. Red was chosen as the predominant color for this area to create a distinct space from the more serious office environment and to encourage relaxation.

Any office space must be functional, but a pleasant atmosphere is equally important. In this case, the sense of history and monumentality to the warehouse inspires respect. To create a harmonious whole, furnishings have minimalist design and neutral colors, to reinforce the sense of sobriety of the building. The result is a work floor like a loft, where workers can easily approach one another. The meeting rooms and conference rooms are situated between the department to ensure that workspaces are not too close together and to enable co-workers room to breathe and focus on their jobs.

Architecture:
Dirk van Berkel
Company:
Univar Europe
Furniture supplier:
Lensvelt
Lighting supplier:
Modular

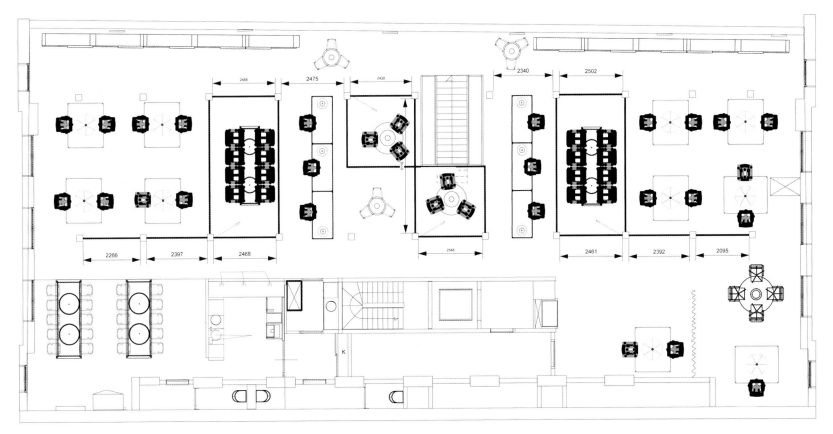

First floor plan

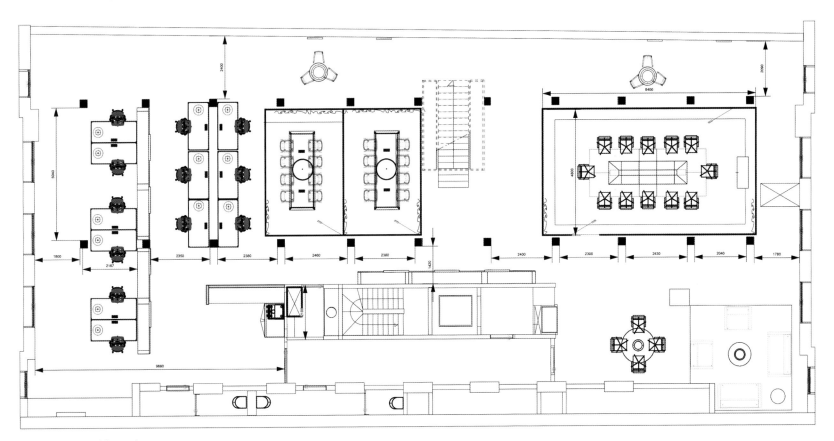

Ground floor plan

The building's listed status imposed a number of limitations on the project to transform the warehouse into new office space. One such restriction was that nothing could be attached to the beams, ceilings and floors. To overcome this, a 'floating' computer system floor was installed, which allows for cables to be wired for each workspace.

The sense of history and monumentality to the warehouse inspires respect. To create a harmonious whole, furnishings have minimalist design and neutral colors, to reinforce the sense of sobriety of the building.

In the left-hand corner at the back of the building is a lunch area with a kitchenette and some tables where the co-workers can have a cup of coffee or some lunch. Red was chosen as the predominant color for this area to create a distinct space from the more serious office environment and to encourage relaxation.

Sid Lee Architecture

Red Bull Amsterdam Headquarters

Amsterdam, The Netherlands

Photographs: Ewout Huibers

Chosen over two other firms, Sid Lee Architecture and Sid Lee's Amsterdam atelier were charged with creating the new Red Bull Amsterdam headquarters. The company agreed to settle on the north side of Amsterdam's port area, in a site evocative of both an artistic street culture and the intensity of extreme sports. The project landed in an old heritage shipbuilding factory, facing a crane and an old disused Russian submarine.

The inner space was designed with the aim of utilizing Red Bull's philosophy to divide spaces according to their use and spirit, suggesting the idea of two opposed and complementary hemispheres of the human mind. Reason contrasts with intuition, art with industry, dark with light, according to Jean Pelland, lead design architect and Senior Partner at Sid Lee Architecture.

Inside the shipbuilding factory, with its three adjacent bays, the architects focused on expressing the dichotomy of space, shifting from public spaces to private ones, from black to white and from white to black.

The goal in this endeavor was to combine the almost brutal simplicity of an industrial building with Red Bull's mystical invitation to perform. The interior architecture with its multiple layers of meaning conveys this dual personality, reminding the user of mountainous cliffs one moment and skate board ramps the next. These triangle shaped piles, as if ripped off the body of a ship, build up semi-open spaces that can be viewed from below, as niches, or from above, as bridges and mezzanines spanning across space. In this architecture, nothing is clearly set; everything is a matter of perception.

Architecture:
Sid Lee Architecture

Client:
Red Bull Netherlands

Visual Identity and Graphics:
Sid Lee

Builders:
Fiction Factory

Furniture:
2D&W

Local Architects (permits):
Kamstra Architecten BNA

General Contractor:
Jora Vision B.V.

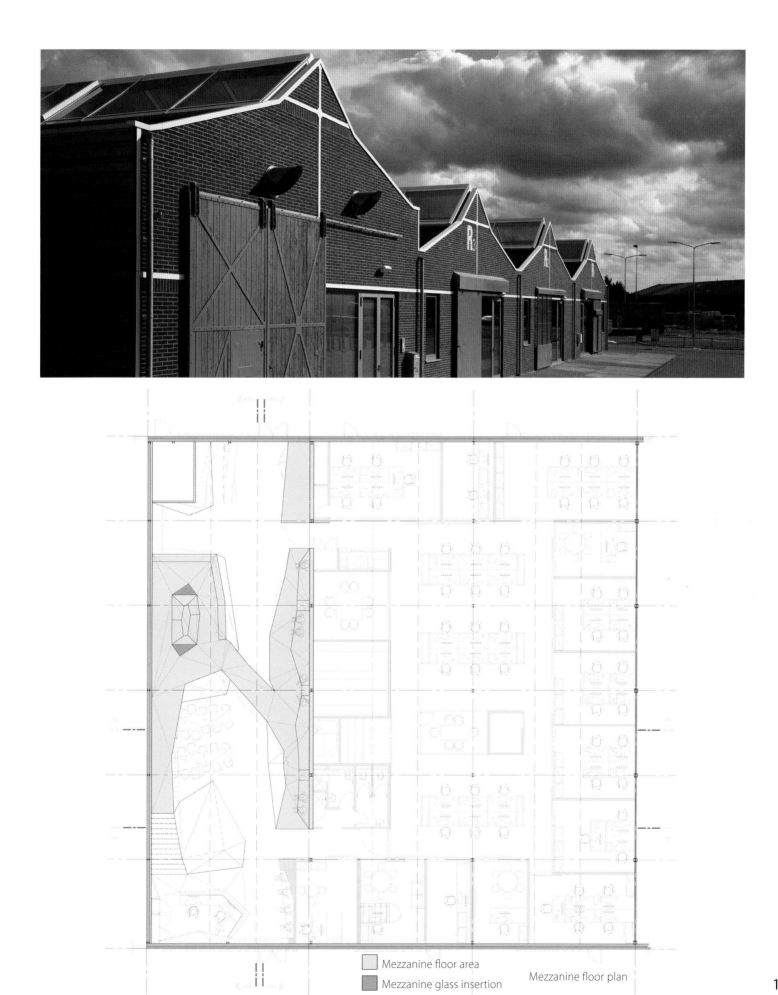

Mezzanine floor area

Mezzanine glass insertion

Mezzanine floor plan

The inner space was designed with the aim of utilizing Red Bull's philosophy to divide spaces according to their use and spirit, suggesting the idea of two opposed and complementary hemispheres of the human mind.

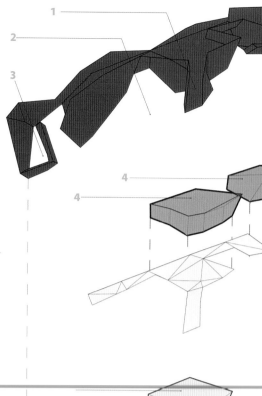

1
2
3
Skin

4
4
Areas 2nd level

2nd level

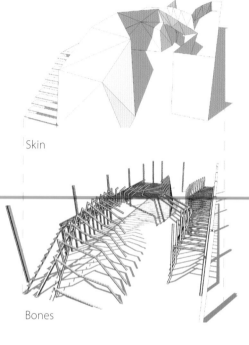

Skin

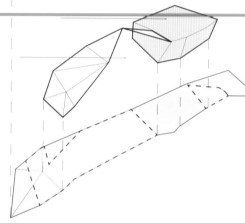

Areas ground level

Ground level

Bones

KEY
1. The crossing
2. The dive
3. The landing
4. Flex space

The interior architecture with its multiple layers of meaning conveys this dual personality, reminding the user of mountainous cliffs one moment and skate board ramps the next. These triangle shaped piles, as if ripped off the body of a ship, build up semi-open spaces that can be viewed from below, as niches, or from above, as bridges and mezzanines spanning across space.

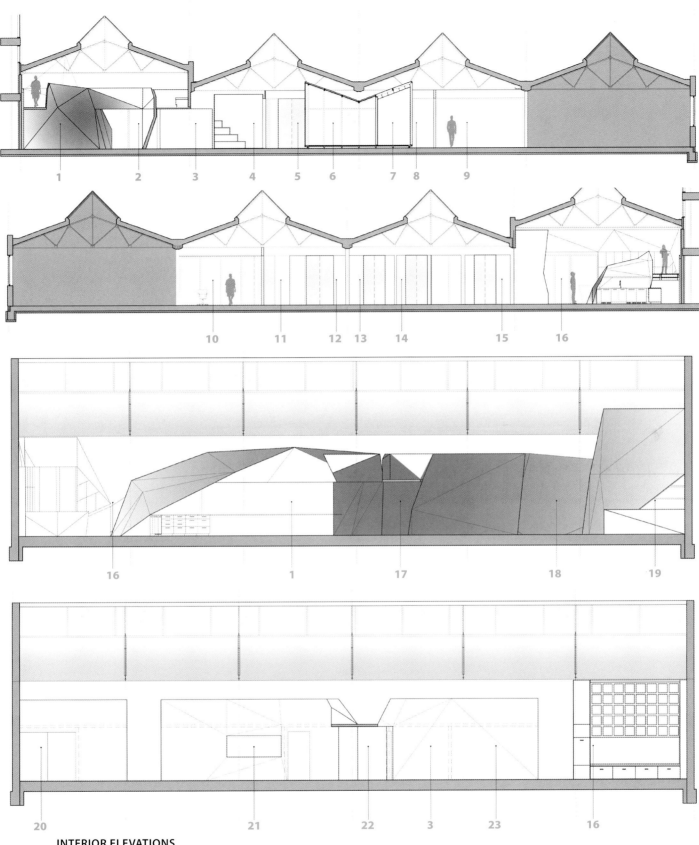

INTERIOR ELEVATIONS

1. 40,90 m² The dive
2. Photo shoot
3. 11,00 m² Quiet room
4. 7,70 m² Quiet room
5. 30,90 m² Operations 5 pers.
6. 10,10 m² Mobile out

7. 4,60 m² Printer room
8. 39,70 m² Finance 5 pers.
9. 20,80 m² Sales 3 pers.
10. Sales 2
11. Sales manager
12. Marketing director

13. MGMT assist.
14. Rooms MT man. dir.
15. HR office
16. The landing
17. Board room
18. Crash room

19. Wet bar
20. Garbage recycle
21. Sound clash
22. Storage
23. Holy shit

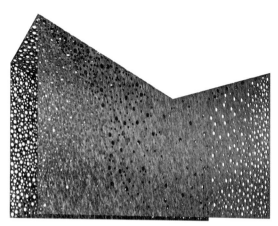

Metal shell

Glass enclosure

Inside the shipbuilding factory, with its three adjacent bays, the architects focused on expressing the dichotomy of space, shifting from public spaces to private ones, from black to white and from white to black.

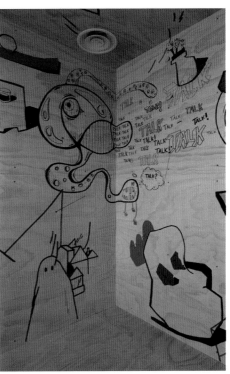

S&T Design Studio

Stephenson and Turner Wellington Studios

Wellington, New Zealand

Photographs: Paul McCredie

Timber floors, brick walls and open trusses provide the backdrop for Stephenson&Turner's new Design Studio in Wellington, New Zealand. Located on the top floor of a 110-year-old building, the open-plan office design speaks to the firm's core philosophy of "creating inspirational environments". Stephenson&Turner is a long-standing multi-disciplinary design firm. The in-house designers specifically chose to refurbish an existing historic space to contrast the relationship between the old and the new, while also creating a stimulating environment for the firm's architects and engineers.

The design studio is on the third floor. Originally there was only stair access, making the space difficult to let and unattractive as office accommodation. A unique solution involved reopening a forgotten connection with the adjacent elevator-serviced building, which coincidentally was designed by Stephenson&Turner in the 1970s. Arriving at Stephenson&Turner is now something of an adventure – the user enters a modern lobby and takes an elevator that progresses through a hole cut in the concrete shear-wall into the timber and brick of the design studio.

The designers decided to break free from open-plan office norms and create a space that would encourage high levels of group communication. Partition screens were eliminated and meeting rooms are the only built spaces in the fit out. They float centrally within the existing shell, shielding the kitchen café space from the open plan studio. Informal meeting spaces are also scattered throughout the studio to facilitate communication, including the café space, which transitions into a well established design library.

This project also showcases the firm's commitment to sustainable architecture and building services engineering. Re-using the existing built environment provided a foundation level of sustainability that went beyond the traditional emphasis on energy efficiency and sustainable materials. A heritage building was preserved for the future and given a new lease on life.

The studio features sustainably harvested and reused timber, daylight addressable lighting, natural ventilation, heat-pump and radiant heating, a green wall and strict use of low VOC paints and adhesives. Focusing on construction waste minimization resulted in 90% of waste materials being recycled or reused.

The light, open-plan environment also encourages and improves health, well-being and productivity. Natural daylight and ventilation is maximized through the use of eight operable skylights, working in conjunction with an intelligent lighting system. Other features include user-controlled fresh air and heating, the separation of utility areas (printers etc.) from the general office space, and various systems to aid in the move the move towards a paperless office environment.

The result is a working environment that is fresh, comfortable, open and airy for both staff and clients.

Architecture:
S&T Design Studio
Project Principal:
Dennis Chippindale
Project Architect:
Malcolm Gardiner
Project Designer:
Matthew Kinsey
Lighting Designer:
Michael Warwick
Client:
Stephenson&Turner New Zealand Ltd.

STEPHENSON
TURNER

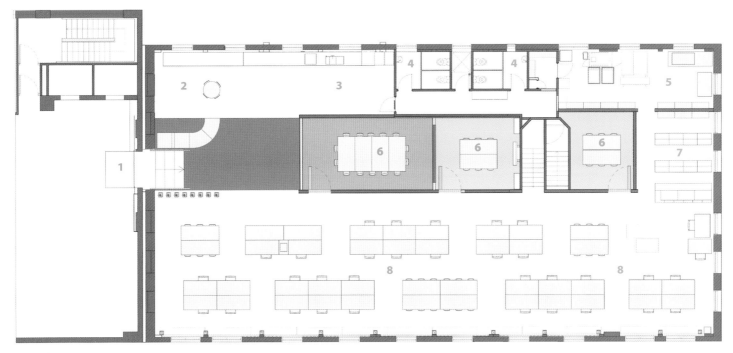

Floor plan

1. Public entrance
2. Cafe
3. Kitchen
4. Toilets
5. Utility/recycling
6. Meeting room
7. Library
8. Open plan office space

Arriving at Stephenson&Turner is now something of an adventure – the user enters a modern lobby and takes an elevator that progresses through a hole cut in the concrete shear-wall into the timber and brick of the design studio.

Informal meeting spaces are also scattered throughout the studio to encourage communication, including the café space, which incorporates a floating linear kitchen, transitioning into a well established design library.

The light, open-plan environment also encourages and improves health, well-being and productivity. Natural daylight and ventilation is maximized through the use of eight operable skylights. These work in conjunction with an intelligent lighting system which adjusts artificial lighting in accordance with the amount of available daylight.

SCOPE Office for Architecture

SAP Office Space For Teams

Walldorf, Germany

Photographs: Zooey Braun

This project involved designing the interior office space on the top two floors of a six floor administration building from the 1990s, and, in doing so, creating an entirely new office concept for the software giant SAP. The client's requirements included a tailor-made concept that would endorse teamwork and support the specific processes of software development. The uncommunicative and insulating cell structure was to be replaced by a bright inspiring space to support employees in their daily tasks, enrich the creative working process, encourage communication and provide the opportunity for concentrated work.

The two floors were completely deconstructed, and redesigned into an H-shaped floor plan, which offers several teams a 'home' in its four wings, with two or three sharing each wing. The needs and demands of programmers in an office environment were analyzed in workshops and staff meetings and taken into account in the built interior. Workspaces are arranged along the window axis and are fit with alternating acoustic baffles in the central zone. The conflict between concentration and communication, always an issue in offices, is resolved with an emphasis on functional built-in spaces. Table groups are livened up through team 'living rooms' or sliding door meetings rooms. The individual workspaces are calmer, whereas communication takes place in think tanks, face-to-face and in programming stations. Here, programmers can jointly discuss solutions and quickly change worskpaces. The central floor space in the H-structure is the marketplace. In contains a cafeteria, a library, two meeting rooms and benches. It is designed as an open room, where presentations can be given to up to 200 people. The presentation area is an elevated platform, with scattered stools for participants and observers. The marketplace is flanked by four areas offering space to services such as a printing room and a games room.

A homelike atmosphere has been created with the use of color and materials. The office walls and floor fixtures are in light oak, accented with white painted surfaces. Many of these areas are magnetic and can be written on, for off-the-cuff creativity. The large glass surfaces that act as soundbreakers between workspaces are painted and have graphic overlays, and can be used as whiteboards. Programming stations are acoustically separated by two-color curtains lined with felt. There are different color schemes for each of the individual wings, to heighten the employee's sense of identification with their environment.

Architecture:
SCOPE Office for Architecture
Client:
SAP AG, Walldorf
Project Team:
Oliver Kettenhofen, Mike Herud, Mike Müller
Graphics:
SCHMID DESIGN
Lighting Consultant:
Henn-PlanungsWerkstatt
Project Management:
INGENIEURBÜRO STEHRENBERG,
Engineer:
K+P GmbH
Plumbing (MEP) Engineer:
pit Plan GmbH,
Acoustical Engineer:
GN Bauphysik Ingenieurgesellschaft mbH
Net building area:
4,800 sqm (51,700 sqft)
Gross floor area:
5,400 sqm (58,100 sqft)

The two floors were completely deconstructed, and redesigned into an H-shaped floor plan, which offers several teams a 'home' in its four wings, with two or three sharing each wing.

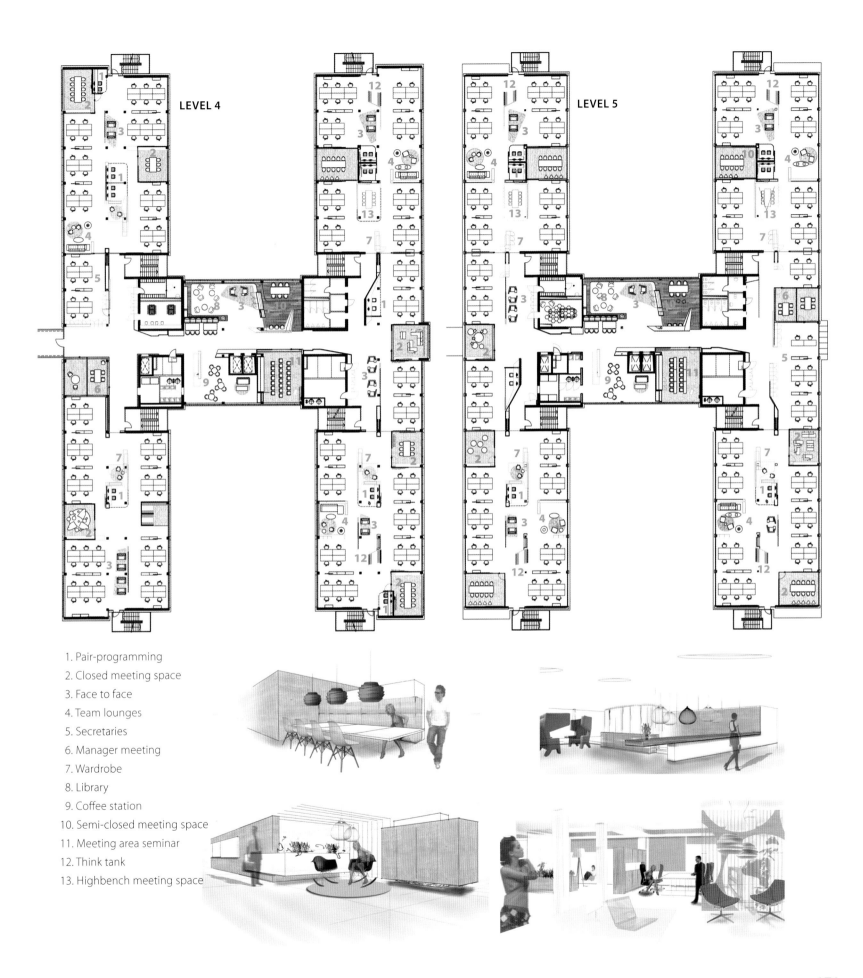

LEVEL 4

LEVEL 5

1. Pair-programming
2. Closed meeting space
3. Face to face
4. Team lounges
5. Secretaries
6. Manager meeting
7. Wardrobe
8. Library
9. Coffee station
10. Semi-closed meeting space
11. Meeting area seminar
12. Think tank
13. Highbench meeting space

The conflict between concentration and communication, always an issue in offices, is resolved with an emphasis on functional built-in spaces. Table groups are livened up through team 'living rooms' or sliding door meetings rooms. The individual workspaces are calmer, whereas communication takes place in think tanks, face-to-face and in programming stations.

A homelike atmosphere has been created with the use of color and materials. The office walls and floor fixtures are in light oak, accented with white painted surfaces.

Lemay

Astral Media Offices

Montreal, Canada

Photograph: Claude-Simon Langlois

In the spring of 2010, Astral Media relocated approximately 350 employees to four floors of a downtown Montreal building. The goals of this large-scale project included elaborating new furniture standards, fitting up flexible meeting spaces and optimizing employee interconnectivity in a contemporary, energetic and versatile working environment.

Based on the client's four different business units (radio, television, advertising and digital media), the architects' concept was inspired by key broadcasting industry words such as influence, communication, movement and exchange. Graphic and signage interventions were incorporated into the project's design from the get-go. These elements are an integral and indivisible part of the space and animate the environment while giving it purpose, personality and functionality. The concept plays on the contrast between medium and message and manifests itself in undulating and pixelated graphics.

In addition to closed offices and workstation, the space incorporates a large conference center which includes meeting and videoconferencing rooms, a main reception area, and listening rooms, in addition to common services (dining room, lounge, café, copy center, etc.). In order to create a rhythm and a gradation throughout the playful 6,000 sqm (64,600 sqft) space, each floor is identified by its own colour and the levels are linked by a central glass staircase.

The client's offices are located in a building which obtained, thanks in part to Astral's efforts, BOMA Best certification, indicating a low environmental impact. By selecting energy efficient lighting equipment and rationalizing electricity needs, this refurbishment succeeded in lowering the client's energy consumption in order to obtain a level 2 certification. Recycling bins were dispersed strategically throughout the space to facilitate access to users who have no excuse not to recycle and all demolition work was executed ecologically (certified). Moreover, the project's layout provides access to daylight for all: open workstations are arranged along the building's perimeter and the closed offices, located near the core, feature floor-to-ceiling glass façades.

The project's main challenges consisted in rejuvenating the client's brand and accommodating a large number of previously dispersed employees in a single open and standardized space, while being mindful of generational differences in the staff makeup. The design team envisioned the project as an opportunity for Astral Media to affirm its role as a leader in the media industry by creating a working environment that reflected its values and new brand image.

Aside from the ingenious use of graphics, light and colour to express Astral's new identity, the project's creativity is also expressed through clever space usage. The result: a compact but ultra-functional working environment accommodating formal and informal meeting spaces such as cafés, meeting rooms, an auditorium and a game room, all linked by the central glass stairway, the spine of the entire project. This is all a means to an end--to incite more interaction between the different business units and promote impromptu exchanges between employees.

Architecture:
Louis T. Lemay (Partner in Charge);
Sandra Neill (designer, associate);
Chantal Ladrie (Project Manager);
François Descôteaux, Isabelle Matte,
Serge Tremblay, Caroline Lemay (Designers);
Marie-Élaine Globensky,
Véronique Richard (Graphic Designers)

Flooring:
Ceragrès

Lighting:
LumiGroup and Axis

Graphics:
LAMCOM Technologies inc.

Furniture:
Nemus, Herman Miller, Knoll,
CIME and Steelcase

Area:
6,000 sqm (64,600 sqft)

17 floor

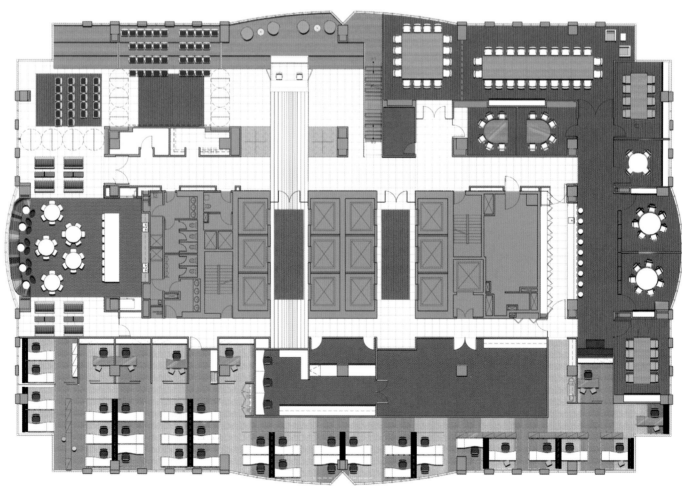

16 floor

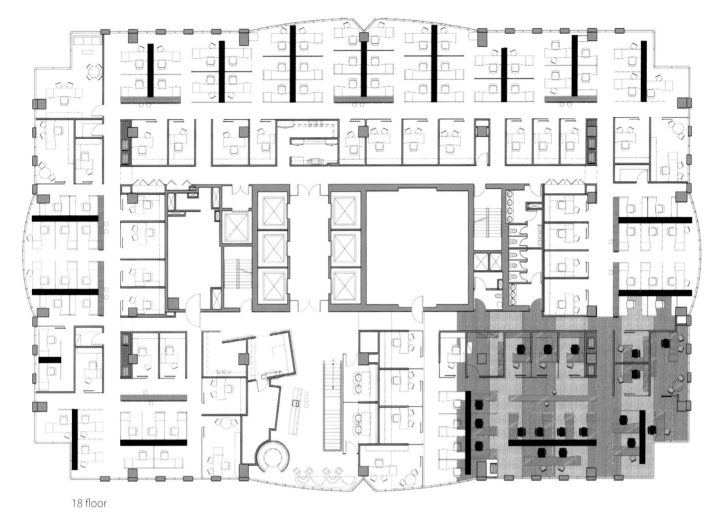

18 floor

179

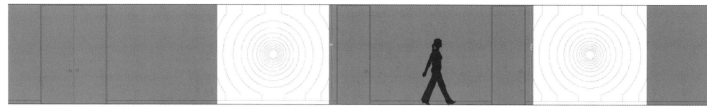

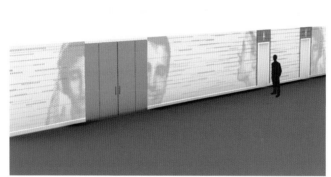

Graphic and signage interventions were incorporated into the project's design from the get-go. These elements are an integral and indivisible part of the space and animate the environment while giving it purpose, personality and functionality. The concept plays on the contrast between medium and message and manifests itself in undulating and pixelated graphics.

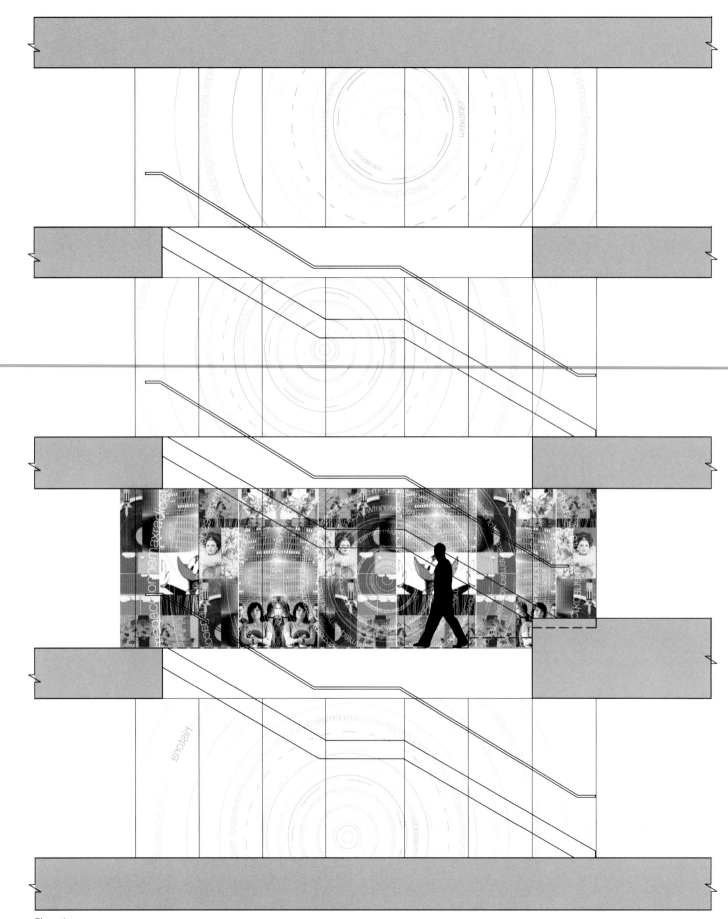

Elevation

In order to create a rhythm and a gradation throughout the playful 6,000 sqm (64,600 sqft) space, each floor is identified by its own colour and the levels are linked by a central glass staircase.

The project's layout provides access to daylight for all: open workstations are arranged along the building's perimeter and the closed offices, located near the core, feature floor-to-ceiling glass façades.

Daz Architects

Ayna head offices

Beirut, Lebanon

Photographs: Diane Aftimos

Located in the central district of Beirut, Ayna Head Offices occupy the top three floors of an existing building. The brief was to amalgamate separate offices into one central headquarters. Priorities included encouraging interaction between employees, and the designers aimed to realize Ayna Head Offices as an urban park. The three floors act as social urban hub containing the main city components: piazza-meeting place, landscape, industrial storage, electrical rooms, football court, public library, road signs and mirrors, public toilets and so on. They are in continual use throughout the day, for company activities and encouraging interaction.

The designers decided not to divide the space with permanent partitions but to create spaces by placing urban elements on each level, a strategy which is not often used on this scale. In many aspects the Ayna offices are best characterized as a covered outside space.

The new panoramic elevator that connects the three floors is contained in a glass box in the middle of the space that reflects the communication between all departments. Meanwhile the conference rooms, centered in the middle of each floor suggest a sense of transparency and openness to ideas and imagination. Glass walls offer 360 degree of transparency with interior curtains: privacy without exclusivity. The space is strongly structured around the visible conference room "Network communication".

Modern materials were chosen, such as plastic, stamped concrete, exposed ducts, contemporary colors, galvanized and brushed steel to raise contrasts with the industrial character of the conference room. The columns and ceiling are in rough concrete.

All these elements come together to achieve a common objective: a work environment that is modern and full of city features. In short: the ideal office.

Architecture:
Daz Architects
Engineering:
Wissam Hobeika, Elie Sobhieh
Lighting:
DIB (Design In Beirut)
Furniture:
OWC (Office Work Center)
Contractor:
C.C.I (Compagnie de construction immobilière)

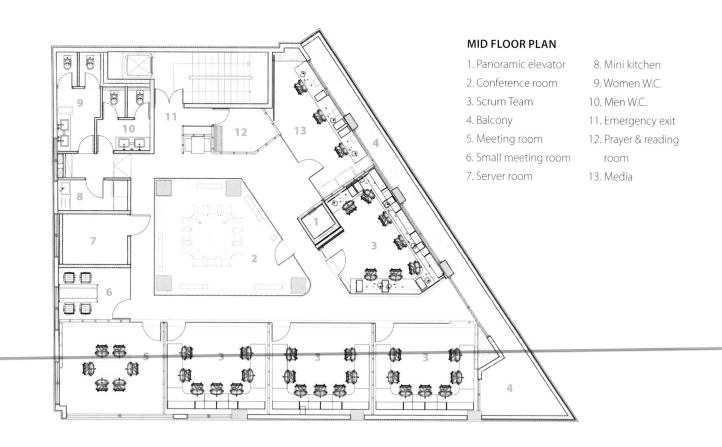

MID FLOOR PLAN

1. Panoramic elevator	8. Mini kitchen
2. Conference room	9. Women W.C.
3. Scrum Team	10. Men W.C.
4. Balcony	11. Emergency exit
5. Meeting room	12. Prayer & reading
6. Small meeting room	room
7. Server room	13. Media

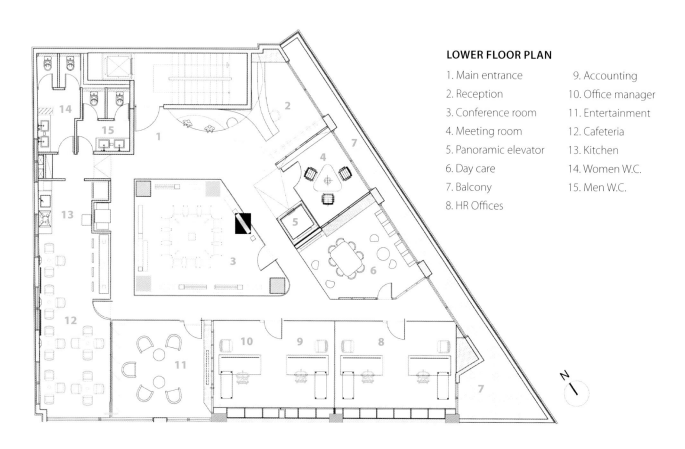

LOWER FLOOR PLAN

1. Main entrance	9. Accounting
2. Reception	10. Office manager
3. Conference room	11. Entertainment
4. Meeting room	12. Cafeteria
5. Panoramic elevator	13. Kitchen
6. Day care	14. Women W.C.
7. Balcony	15. Men W.C.
8. HR Offices	

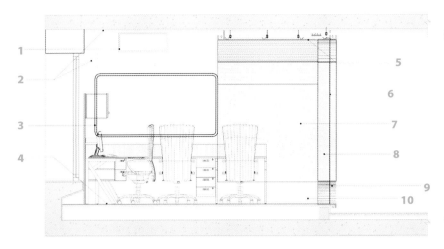

SECTION

1. Ducts
2. Plaster to receive paint
3. Board
4. Ceramic
5. Gypsum board
6. Glass
7. Gypsum board
8. Gypsum board
9. Metal Plate 6 mm
10. Plaster to receive paint

INTERIOR ELEVATION

1. Mirror
2. Panel board
3. Tiling
4. Technomarble
5. Melamine wood
6. PVC Skirting
7. Microwave

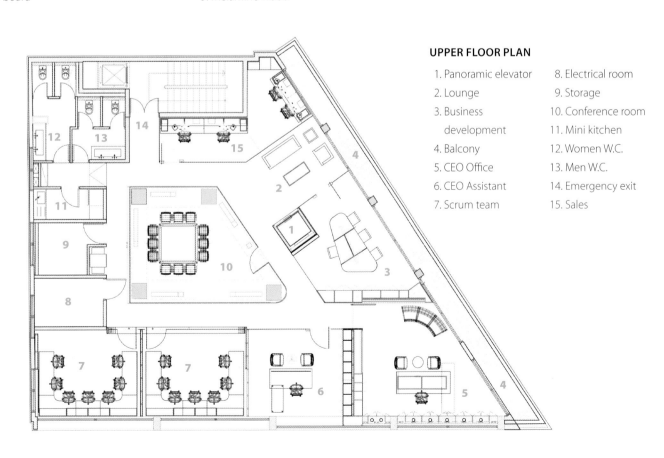

UPPER FLOOR PLAN

1. Panoramic elevator
2. Lounge
3. Business development
4. Balcony
5. CEO Office
6. CEO Assistant
7. Scrum team
8. Electrical room
9. Storage
10. Conference room
11. Mini kitchen
12. Women W.C.
13. Men W.C.
14. Emergency exit
15. Sales

Glass walls offer 360 degree of transparency with interior curtains: privacy without exclusivity. The space is strongly structured around the visible conference room "Network communication".

The designers decided not to divide the space with permanent partitions but to create spaces by placing urban elements on each level, a strategy which is not often used on this scale.

COMODO Interior & Furniture Design Co. Ltd.

Comodo Office, "Landscape in Bustling City"

Hong Kong, China

Photographs: contributed by the designers

Interior design always works within boundaries and has been hidden in bustling city landscape. Because of these boundaries, the connections between internal spaces, people and the city landscape have been segregated. In this project, the designer wanted to put emphasis on such connections and therefore used point-to-point method to define internal landscape and to re-create linkages to connect internal design, people and city landscape back together.

The internal landscape goes with the spatial arrangement from two sides forming the platform and partitions, along to and connected as a whole at the end side. The designer used wooden materials and light wood color, in contrast to the tall and compact city landscape. Altogether, the internal landscape, wooden materials and natural light create a natural and comfortable working environment, and expose the connections into the bustling city.

The open-plan work area is located close to the windows. Natural light streams in through the windows making the room bright and warm, while the pleasant environment encourages the workers to produce creative designs. Glass partitions clearly divide the space of conference room but still keep the plan open and give the space a sense of flow. The materials room is next to the conference room, with a sliding door in between. When the door is open, the sliding door leaves just enough room for the book cabinet at the corner. A few leisure areas, some with sofas and coffee tables, are located at corners of the studio, for entertaining guests and even enjoying a little leisure moment besides intense work tasks.

The lighting is largely natural, but spot lights are also minimally employed over the office. There are two decorative pendent lights in the conference room, three above the pantry table and one above the bar table.

Design Company:
COMODO Interior & Furniture Design Co. Ltd.
Designer:
Alain Wong

In this project, the designer wanted to put emphasis on such connections and therefore used point-to-point method to define internal landscape and to re-create linkages to connect internal design, people and city landscape back together.

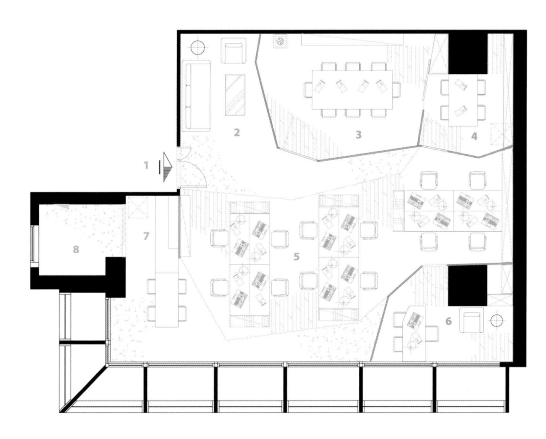

FLOOR PLAN

1. Entrance
2. Reception/waiting area
3. Meeting room A
4. Material room
5. Working area
6. Director room
7. Pantry
8. Store room

id+s Design Solutions

Astral Media Offices

Montreal, Quebec, Canada

Photographs: Claude-Simon Langlois

Astral is one of Canada's largest media companies. Its roots in media trace back to Montreal's Greenberg brothers, who created a photography chain 50 years ago. Adopting a new brand identity reflecting the company's evolving culture, along with a move of their headquarters in the heart of downtown Montreal, required the 1,700 sqm (18,500 sqft) executive floor to be representative of this new vibrant culture and also reflective of the founder's personality and wishes of a warm, comfortable and elegant workspace. Working hand in hand with the founder made this a unique and memorable design process. The design challenge was to create a warm, comfortable and "established" executive floor, amidst a highly modern media company identified on the other 5 floors. The warm light oak flooring and paneling is reminiscent of the finishes of the 80s, but contrasts with the crisp white walls and dark glass. The effect serves to simplify, and yet at the same time warm the space. Red was used as an accent, not only for its vibrancy, but also for its contemporaneity and timelessness. Graphic walls were introduced sparingly to inject color and whimsy into the space.

Space restraints meant that accommodating executive window offices, large conference rooms, and a naturally lit reception area was problematic. The solution was to stretch the space horizontally to reach out to the windows of the executive work areas in both directions of the building. The horizontality is emphasized by a "waved" feature wall that serves as a backdrop to the main desk, and allows for glimpses of daylight. During brainstorming sessions, employees unanimously agreed that Astral´s founder is a very jovial, approachable man who is a natural "people person", and that being geographically disconnected on the executive floor from his team and conference rooms was isolating him. Today, his floor not only reflects his personality and the values and roots of the firm, but allows employees on all floors to feel the warmth of his welcome.

Designers:
id+s Design Solutions Inc.
Project leader:
Susie Silveri
Design team:
Anne-Marie Charlebois,
project designer and coordinator,
Chantal Lusignan,
project coordinator / technical drawings
Architect:
Richard Alpha
Engineers:
Planifitech
Contractor:
Patella Construction
Surface area:
1,700 sqm (18,000 sqft)

Space restraints meant that accommodating executive window offices, large conference rooms, and a naturally lit reception area was problematic. The solution was to stretch the reception horizontally to reach out to the windows of the executive work areas in both directions of the building.

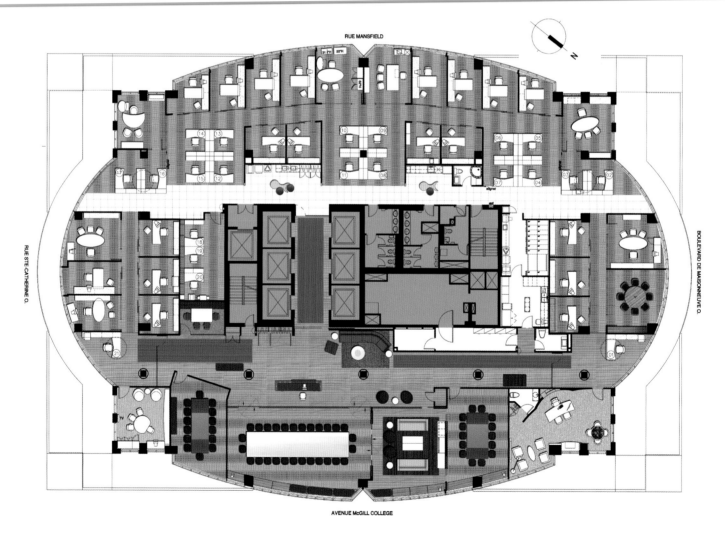

Floor plan

204

The warm light oak flooring and paneling is reminiscent of the finishes of the 80s, but contrasts with the crisp white walls and dark glass. The effect serves to simplify, and yet at the same time warm the space. Red was used as an accent, not only for its vibrancy, but also for its contemporaneity and timelessness.

Sander Architecten

Rabobank Nederland Offices

Utrecht, the Netherlands

Photographs: Alexander van Berge, Ray Edgar

Having completed the Square, a new office building for Rabobank Nederland in Utrecht, Sander Architecten were selected by the clients from among twenty practices to create and supervise the execution of the interior design of the 56,000 sqm (603,000 sqft) complex comprising the Square and a twenty-five story office tower.

Sander Architecten envisaged the office building as a modern city, creating an environment in which employees and visitors work, eat, read, and meet one another in a diverse landscape. Spaces with different functions interact within a grid of skylights and slender columns.

The new style of working is based on freedom, trust and taking responsibility. Rabobank sees its employees as entrepreneurs, responsible for their own performance in an environment free of fixed rules, fixed times and fixed locations. The workspaces accommodate a defined set of activities: whether multi-person meetings, one-on-one meetings or concentrated individual work, each activity has its own space.

In the design of the circulation spaces throughout the office, the architects sought to uncover and reinforce the natural flow of the workers as they moved through their working day. The busiest points are those closest to the elevators and staircases, beyond which more peaceful zones naturally emerged. The architects understood the concept of flow as the moment when need, desire and ability come together, hence they believed that optimizing the natural flow of people would be beneficial for the employees' sense of happiness as well as their productivity. The guiding principle for the interior design therefore became 'form follows flow'. Vertical partitions were avoided so that the horizon would always be visible.

Meeting pavilions made from washi paper and paperboard combine with washi paper Chinese lanterns suspended from the skylight to create a rich textural experience. The paperboard pavilions, which feature attractive patterns created by using the material in different ways, are particularly tactile.

Architecture:
Sander Architecten
Client:
Rabobank Nederland

Sander Architecten envisaged the office building as a modern city, creating an environment in which employees and visitors work, eat, read, and meet one another in a diverse landscape.

Sander Architecten sought to uncover and re-inforce the natural flow of employees as they moved through their day. Understanding the concept of flow as the moment when need, de-sire and ability come together, the architects be-lieved that optimizing the natural flow of people would be beneficial for the employees' sense of happiness as well as for their productivity.

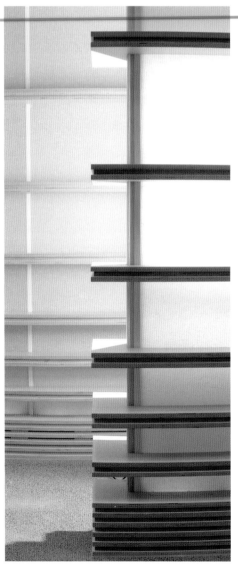

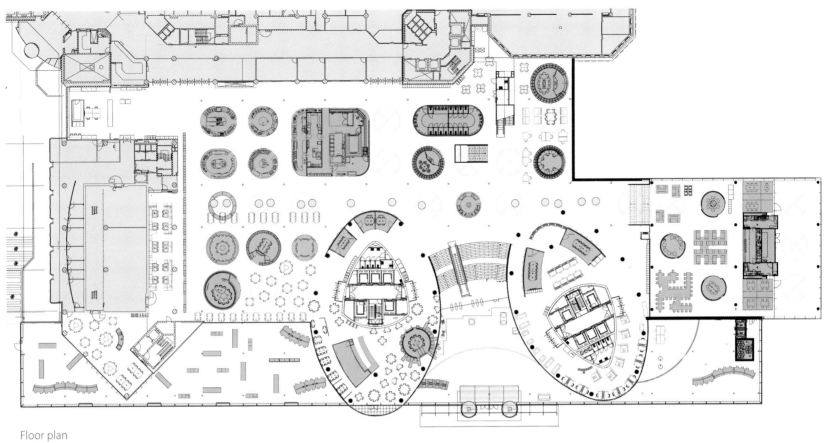

Floor plan

215

gullsten-inkinen

V Kontakte Offices

St. Petersburg, Russia

Photographs: contributed by the architects

V Kontakte is a Russian social media site. It operates in the former Soviet region and has currently 100 million users, approximately 70% of whom are within Russia. The young staff wanted more informality and fewer traditional and formal workspaces. The design concept was "an industrial warehouse" and the challenge was to convey this theme within a new building.

During the design process, V Konkakte staff ran with the inside joke of wanting walls with concrete effect wall-paper, as real concrete walls are currently a trend in "industrial chic" design. The resulting space has contains some brick walls that are similar in appearance to those on the outside of the building. The bricks were deliberately left exposed to play up the industrial theme and to give the workspace a slightly "kitsch" appearance.

The new offices premises are for the most part open-plan, which meant that attention to acoustic details was critical to the success of the design. GI are experts in achieving nearly silent open spaces, and they began by installing carpets throughout, as the majority of the staff are young women with high heeled shoes. There are a variety of spaces planned within the office, from phone booths to silent areas, meetings rooms and play areas.

Despite a dark color palette on walls and ceilings, the spaces are not dark or gloomy. To add a touch of brightness, playful colors and features have been added in the form of furniture, rugs and artwork. There are also reflective finishes: splashes of white on ceilings and walls within specific areas to add brightness to the whole.

To reinforce the idea that this is a company involved in social media and social networking, large scale prints of people's faces have been hung, in images that are relatively abstract close up, but easily identifiable from a distance. The user-driven focus and careful attention to detail strongly incorporates the company's image and brand.

Architecture:
gullsten-inkinen

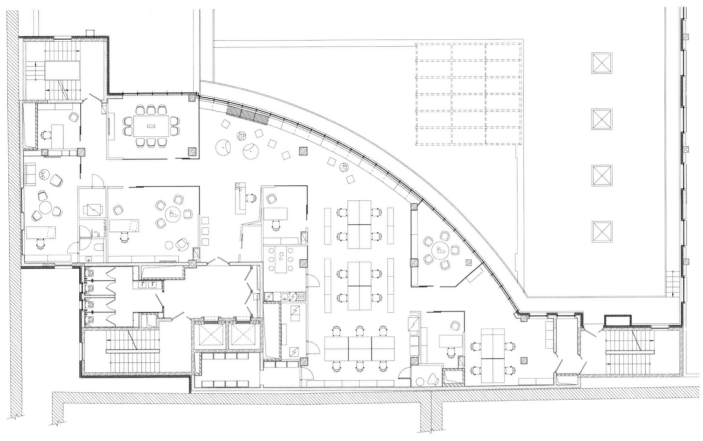

Upper floor plan

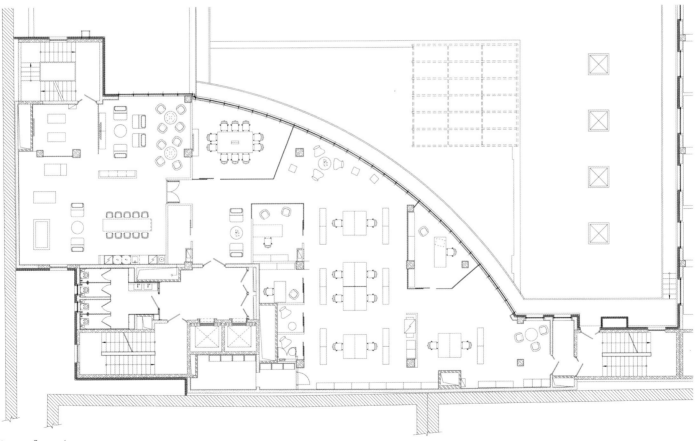

Lower floor plan

Despite a dark color palette on walls and ceilings, the spaces are not dark or gloomy. To add a touch of brightness, playful colors and features have been added in the form of furniture, rugs and artwork.

OpenAD

Inspired Office

Riga, Latvia

Photographs: Maris Lagzdins, Krists Spruksts

The McCann Inspired offices in Riga, Latvia, developed architects OpenAD´s interest in the stylization and union of inner rooms with an exterior aspect. The offices are arranged into "streets," separated into blocks of "houses," fully fitted with windows, façades, podiums and in-floor recessed flower beds. These features contribute to a sense of community but also of comfort, fostering a creative environment with optimal communication between staff. For those who need a break from the community-style, a dome shaped "egg of silence" provides breathing space.

Simple materials have been used throughout: wooden boards, lacquered MDF panels, and plasterboard. The emphasis on the interior decoration was reused and recycled materials, such as the lamps, which are made of wide plasterboard tubes that had previously been used as fabric rolls. This is a low budget project that refuses to sacrifice design credentials to budget but instead works creates an atmosphere that recalls the trendy "trash style" in interior projects.

Arquitecture:
OPEN ARCHITECTURE AND DESIGN
Zane Tetere, Rita Saldeniece
Design:
Elina Tetere
Client:
McCann Erickson-Riga y Inspired
Collaborators:
Edgars Spridzans, artist
LB construction, carpenters
Area:
Inspired: 380 sqm (4,100 sqft) (third floor)
McCann: 640 sqm (6,900 sqft) (fourth floor)
Total area:
1,020 sqm (11,000 sqft)

OpenAD conceived the design for the McCann-Inspired offices, in Riga, Latvia, as the stylized union between interior and exterior, in which the design resembles streets with blocks of houses.

GROUND FLOOR PLAN

1. Entrance
2. Kitchen
3. Brainstorm room
4. Podium workspace
5. Meeting room
6. Egg of silence

The city style layout fosters a sense of community but also of comfort, leading to a creative environment with optimal communication between staff. For those who need a break from the community feel from time to time, a dome shaped "egg of silence" provides breathing space.

The lamps are also made of recycled materials, specifically of plaster tubes which were previously used for holding rolls of cloth.

Shimoda Design Group

Fashion Accessories Office

Southern California, USA

Photographs: contributd by the architects

The main goal of this project is to authentically reflect the spirit and intent of the company's core values. They have a successful business model that combines a for-profit business with an operation that donates their product to those in need.

The spirit of the company is rooted in humility and a do-it-yourself attitude, which extended to a wish to minimize materials and build only what was needed. The company founder and designer met and agreed on a non-corporate vision that would celebrate the company's authentic spirit.

Three things that we specifically addressed were HVAC, drywall, and furniture. It was decided not to air condition the main gathering space, as the original had no cooling and barely had heating. The use of drywall was minimized to 75% of the normal amount provided in typical construction. It was only used in areas where actual work happens, between 3 ft and 7ft off the ground. Additionally, only one side of the wall was clad. Furniture design was minimal, and old furniture was extensively reused. The architects created a system utilizing particle board (no electrified panels) and simple metal and mdf top work desks. Partition modules allowed the reuse and relocation of 125 desks and chairs.

Building materials are humble and unadorned: reclaimed lumber, galvanized structural steel and studs, cork board, white board, wood and concrete, all left in their natural raw state.

The design also sought to connect employees with the outdoors. The previous office had had a tiny alley that was its social heart. This alley was recreated for the new offices in the truck loading dock. The importance of being outside has been underscored by creating abundant outdoor workspace. The team created two giant steel canopies for work and play. There are picnic tables, ping pong tables, a bandstand / DJ stage, bocce ball court and canvas pup tents that are used for conference rooms and team lunches. The outdoor spaces are edged with fruit trees and artificial turf (a material selection based on the lack of rainfall in Southern California). The outdoor space also includes a dog run and access to a yoga studio. Each Monday there is an organic PRODUCT market for the staff to purchase farm fresh food.

Finally, the design aims to bring people together. There are small individual work areas but very large social areas. The outdoor spaces are augmented by a main communal area where bi-monthly "all staff" meetings are held. This area includes conference rooms, a stage, high school gym style bleachers and a coffee bar. Two giant roll up doors connect the interior with the exterior. These areas, when combined, allow for up to 500 people to gather for work or play.

Architecture:
Shimoda Design Group
Architect:
Joey Shimoda AIA, Principal
Project Manger:
Todd Tuntland
Project Team:
Susan Chang, Ying-Ling Sun, Elizabeth Cao,
Romiar Karamooz, Andre Krause,
David Khuong, Dan Allen, Neil Muntzel,
McKenna Cole
Structural Engineer:
John Labib + Associates
**Mechanical, Eletrical and
Plumbing Engineer:**
ARC Engineering
Landscape Architect:
YLS Landscape Architecture
General Contractor:
Corporate Contractors
Area:
78,500 sqft (7,300 sqm)

The previous office had had a tiny alley that was its social heart. This alley was recreted for the new offices in the truck loading dock area.

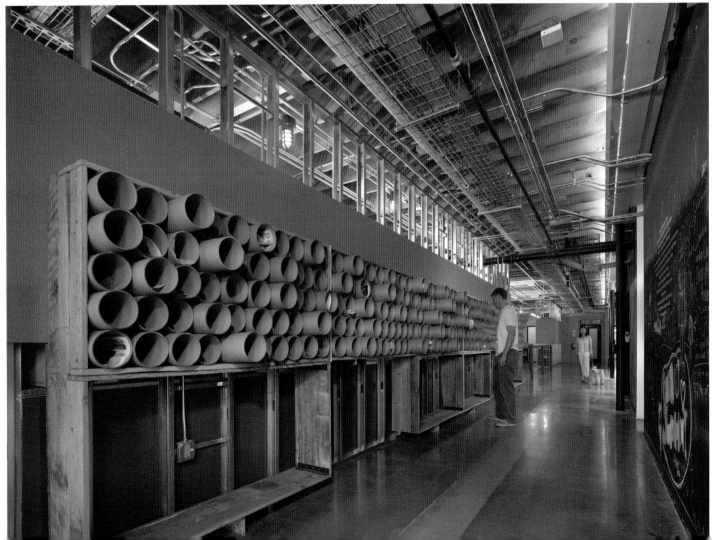

Furniture design was minimal, and old furniture was extensively reused. The architects created a system utilizing particle board (no electrified panels) and simple metal and mdf top work desks. Partition modules allowed the reuse and re-location of 125 desks and chairs.

Building materials are humble and unadorned: reclaimed lumber, galvanized structural steel and studs, cork board, white board, wood and concrete, all left in their natural raw state.

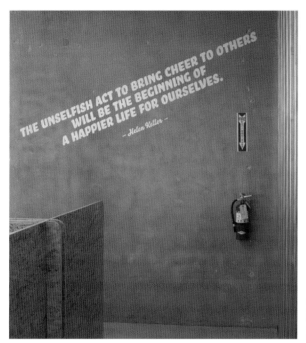

KAMP Arhitektid

Universal Music Finland

Helsinki, Finland

Photographs: Terje Ugandi

The new office of Universal Music of Finland is situated in what were formerly factory rooms. These rooms have been used at different times as a Nokia cable factory, an Airam lighting factory, as a cigarette production space, and most recently as a print shop. Nowadays, due to the building's location next to Länsisatama harbor near Helsinki city center, it holds a number of creative companies – advertisement offices, design furniture companies, design shops, cafes, etc.

The 2-story high room, painted stark white, provided a masculine base, with high windows, concrete surfaces, and massive beams and columns. The architect's plan was to preserve this strong factory atmosphere, even to emphasize it, while at the same time adding some glamour to the room.

Most of the room has remained white, though the floors are now black and largely carpeted. The managing director's room on the second floor is entirely black and has a full view over the office. Large, white 3-D letters hand-cut from insulation foam can be seen from the street, and spell out "Universal Music". On the inside, one of the most immediately noticeable features in the room are the chandeliers made of drum cymbals, giving a clear hint as to the nature of the company. Each 1.5 m (5 ft) wide chandelier is made of 20 cymbals, which glow warmly under the high ceiling.

As listening to music is one of the main components to working in the office, the project included very strict needs for acoustic quality in the offices. In some rooms, all materials have been chosen with sound absorption characteristics, so as to achieve an optimally quiet atmosphere for listening or playing music, or indeed, holding a meeting.

To distinguish the Finnish headquarters from the many other Universal Music offices around the world, touches of northern spirit, such as the use of natural wood and felt, have been infused into the design. There has also been an emphasis on recycling and reusing. 10-year-old office chairs (originally designed by Yrjö Kukkapuro) were taken to Tallinn, Estonia and renovated for the new offices. Ceiling lamps in the open office were made of soviet-era Estonian vinyl records.

Graphic design is very important in the interior spaces. Glass walls are decorated with graphics that play with the remaining factory atmosphere. Glass tables have graphics of old gramophones and a simplified history of music recording, which were designed by Martin Eelma of Tuumik Stuudio.

Architecture:
KAMP Arhitektid
Client:
Universal Music OY
Graphics:
Martin Eelma (Tuumik Stuudio)
Area:
570 sqm (6,100 sqft)

238

The new office of Universal Music of Finland is situated in what were formerly factory rooms. In some rooms, all materials have been chosen with sound absorption characteristics, so as to achieve an optimally quiet atmosphere for listening or playing music, or indeed, holding a meeting.

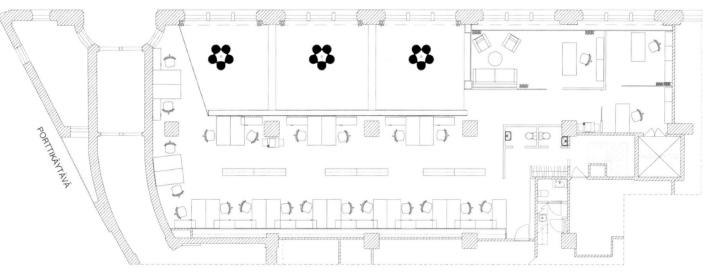

First floor

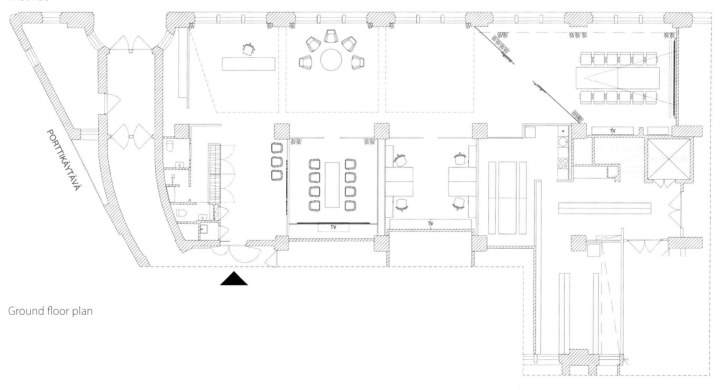

Ground floor plan

To distinguish the Finnish headquarters from the many other Universal Music offices around the world, touches of northern spirit, such as the use of natural wood and felt, have been infused into the design

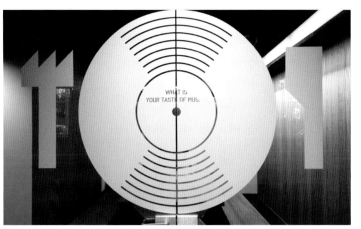

NFOE et associés architectes

Bureau 100

Montreal, Quebec, Canada

Photographs: Stéphane Brügger

NFOE et associés architectes, founded in 1912, recently moved its offices into Old Montreal. The building, the first skyscraper in Montreal – better known as the New York Life Building (1887–89) – stands out from its surroundings for its exuberant Scottish red sandstone and red granite cladding.

Situated in the heart of the city, Bureau 100 is surrounded by several large projects associated with Barott, who orginally founded the company, including the majestic Aldred Building (designed by Barott in 1929 and regarded by many as his most accomplished work), the modernist high rise for the Bank of Montreal's head office, the Royal Trust Building and the National Bank of Canada Building.

A successful synergistic relationship with the owner (winner of the CIGM Commercial Heritage Building Award in 2005) resulted in a large-scale restoration project on the first two floors, occupied by NFOE. The interior, which had deteriorated considerably, was returned to its original state, with impressive Corinthian columns, ornate ceiling moldings, and original woodwork. With immense windows and light colors, the new space is a stimulating work environment.

The project links past and present in a subtle play between verticals and horizontals. Both floors have been freed from partitions. The simple, elegant furnishings act as a background for an architecturally rich and detailed space. The workstations in the open-plan space encourage interaction, while offering the possibility for individual thought and reflection. Zones for improvised meetings are located near workstations. Open spaces emphasize the original ornamentations of the columns, ceilings, moldings, and woodwork. The bank vault is still in place on the ground floor and is now used as a library.

Each floor has a distinct atmosphere: the ground floor is grandiose, whereas the upper floor is intimate. The ground floor has a high (5m/17ft) ceiling and large windows offering a stunning view of Old Montreal. Natural light is diffused into the workspace. The second floor has a lower ceiling, encouraging more intimacy. A series of superimposed drop ceilings amplifies the height reduction and acts as a series of horizontal slabs contrasting with the vertical columns. The different interventions are composed of pure, minimal lines. There is a dialogue between strength, transparency, and the weight of the materials. There are touches of color in the ground floor waiting area: a green monolith and a metal strip floating on a glass panel stand out against the white classical columns. The original woodwork and fireplace have been preserved in the ground-floor conference room. Above, dark walls amplify the height, and visually detach the ornate moldings from the wall. The contemporary lighting fixtures seem to drop like water from the ceiling.

In the mezzanine, a blue wall spans both floors along the interior stairway behind the workspaces, leads to the second floor and continues the cafeteria.

Architecture:
NFOE et associés architectes
Client:
NFOE et associés architectes
Project manager:
Masa Fukushima / Rafie Sossanpour
Design team:
NFOE team
Construction:
BTL Construction
Area:
1,015 sqm (10,900 sqft)

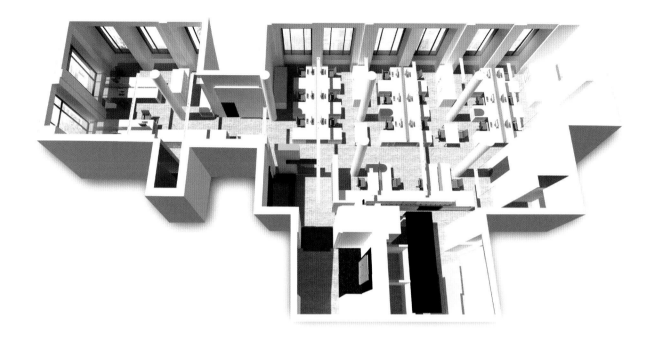

The ground floor is grandiose. There are touches of color in the waiting area: a green monolith and a metal strip floating on a glass panel stand out against the white classical columns. The original woodwork and fireplace have been preserved in the ground-floor conference room. Above, dark walls amplify the height, and visually detach the ornate moldings from the wall. The contemporary lighting fixtures seem to drop like water from the ceiling.

First floor plan

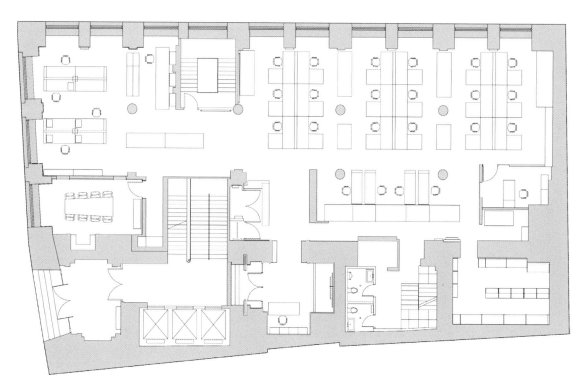

Ground floor plan

The second floor has a lower ceiling, encouraging more intimacy. A series of superimposed drop ceilings amplifies the height reduction and acts as a series of horizontal slabs contrasting with the vertical columns. The different interventions are composed of pure, minimal lines.

Karla Menten

Diamedia Minds Offices

Hasselt, Belgium

Photographs: Philippe van Gelooven

Human relationships and values are central to the work environments of the future. The offices of Diamedia Minds needed to be a social meeting point where specialists and generalists could get together, collaborate and learn from one another. Interaction, communication and cooperation are crucial factors. The office design is aims, therefore, at optimizing interaction, atmosphere, enthusiasm and drive. The sense of working on something together is fundamental, and is emphasized by the open space and the circles in the floor, which lend the design a sense of playfulness and fun, whilst at the same time optimizing the communication and productiveness between different members of a team.

The design has nothing to do with hierarchy. It's about openness and flexibility.

Emphasis is placed on communal areas, on spots conducive to meeting and working together, such as the glass meeting room, and the circles in the floor that serve as desks.

Rather than determining the image of the office space, technology here is a supportive and nearly invisible aid: it aids in human interaction, but it does not replace it.

Architecture:
Karla Menten
Used materials:
Gyproc, PU
Furniture:
made to measure by Moors nv,
design Karla Menten
Lighting:
Viabizzuno
Walls, painting and curtains:
Lode Mouchaers
Floor area:
105 sqm (1,140 sqft)

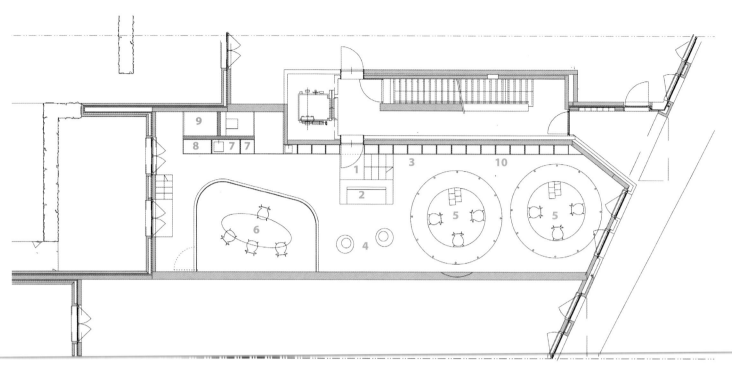

GROUND FLOOR PLAN

1. Entrance
2. Waiting room
3. Lockers
4. Projection wall
5. Workplaces
6. Meeting room
7. Kitchen
8. Printers
9. Servers
10. Archive/storage

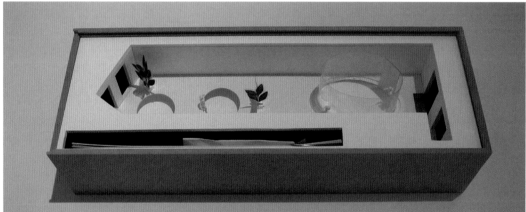

The sense of working on something together is fundamental, and is emphasized by the open space and the circles in the floor. These lend the design a sense of playfulness and fun, whilst at the same time optimizing the communication and productiveness between different members of a team.

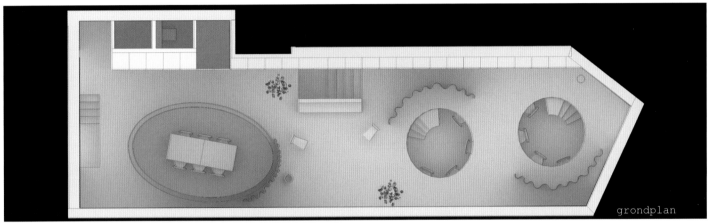

grondplan

doorsn

Human relationships and values are central to the work environments of the future. The offices of Diamedia Minds needed to be a social meeting point where specialists and generalists could get together, collaborate and learn from one another.

Emphasis is placed on communal areas, on spots conducive to meeting and working together, such as the glass meeting room, and the circles in the floor that serve as desks.

i29 l interior architects

Office 04

Amsterdam, the Netherlands

Photographs: contributed by i29 l interior architects

Tribal DDB Amsterdam is a highly ranked digital marketing agency and part of DDB international, worldwide one of the largest advertising offices. i29 interior architects designed their new offices for about 80 people, with an aim to creating an environment where creative interaction is supported and to achieve as much workspace as possible in a new structure with flexible desks and a large open space. Moreover, the architects wished to maintain a work environment that would stimulate long office hours and concentrated work. As Tribal DDB is part of an international network a clear identity was required, which also fits the parent company DDB. The design had to reflect a friendly and playful but also professional and serious identity. The contradictions within these aims dictated choices that would allow flexibility within the design.

As the offices were to be located in a building that could not be entirely structurally changed, it was a challenge to integrate all the desired features into a workable whole. i29 strove to find one grand gesture which could encompass a number of the issues. One priority was to find a material which could be an alternative to the ceiling system, yet would continue to provide cover and to integrate structural parts, like a large, round staircase. Acoustics were also important, given the open spaces and necessary creative interactions. The result was a playful use of fabric. Fabric can be powerful conceptually, is perfect for absorbing sound and can create privacy in open spaces. It was also effectively put to use here covering the scars of demolition. Felt was chosen as the predominant fabric for its versatility — it can be used on floors, ceilings, walls, and to create pieces of furniture and lampshades — its durability, acoustic suitability, and the fact that it is fireproof and environmentally friendly. Nonetheless, producing all of the above items from this one material did present a challenge.

i29 always seeks to answer multiple questions at once: in this case, they have told a conceptual story about the company, the space, and the users of the space. They have dealt with specific practical and functional issues while maintaining an autonomous quality to the work. These 'levels' are intertwined, the intelligent design referring back to the company, an independent powerful image returns to the theme of functionality, and so on. Intermixed with these concepts is i29's belief that simplicity builds character. In design as in life, it can be difficult to stay focused on the most important projects. The result of being very selective is that it is necessary to push that one choice to its limits. This energizes a space without letting it fall into chaos, and more importantly, results in a charismatic environment.

Architecture:
i29 l interior architects
(Jaspar Jansen & Jeroen Dellensen)
Client:
Tribal DDB Amsterdam
Construction:
Slavenburg
Interior construction:
Zwartwoud
Area:
650 sqm (7,000 sqft)

The design had to reflect a friendly and playful but also professional and serious identity. The contradictions within these aims dictated choices that would allow flexibility within the design.

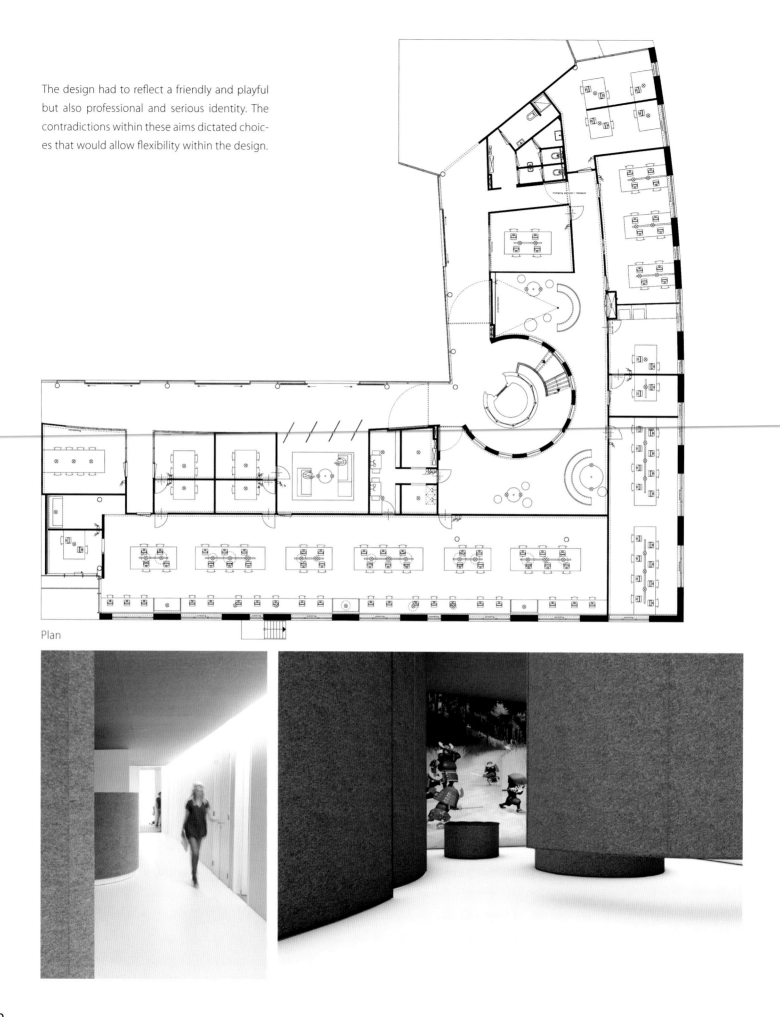

Plan

One priority was to find a material which could be an alternative to the ceiling system, yet would continue to provide cover and to integrate structural parts, like a large, round staircase. Acoustics were also important, given the open spaces and necessary creative interactions. The result was a playful use of fabric. i29 always seeks to answer multiple questions at once: in this case, they have told a conceptual story about the company, the space, and the users of the space.

M Moser Associates

Grace, Space, Place: Societe Generale Private Banking

Central District, Hong Kong, China   **Photographs:** contributed by M Moser Associates

Building new brands is a challenge; but maintaining and evolving a well-established brand is no less stimulating a task for interior designers. In Societe Generale Private Banking's (SGPB's) case, the Group's brand roots reach all the way back to 1864. Though their activities have greatly expanded, their essence, offering wealth management solutions to entrepreneurs and High Net Worth Individuals– with cultural passions in wine, art, golf and cinema – has remained. The offices in Edinburgh Tower, Central district, were refurbished for more space and to upgrade their facilities. M Moser Associates – with whom SGPB had worked on previous projects in Hong Kong – were called upon to carry out the renovation.

The reception is on the 38th floor, and the rest of the design radiates out from this 'anchor': meeting rooms follow, and then the back-of-house. These three layers – reception, meeting rooms, back of house-- correspond with the layers of SGPB's business and how it serves its clients.

From the lifts, visitors step onto a red carpet whose hue echoes that of SGPB's logo and implies VIP treatment. The logo is rendered in a subtle imprint on the wall. The generous dimensions of the reception area are accentuated by a near-total lack of furniture, a disciplined color palette, and a careful composition of sharply defined forms. The reception desk itself is a monolithic structure whose black marble base and white marble top appear to have been horizontally bisected. A thin protruding lip between the two elements shows the desk to be another adventurous play on the SGPB logo. Identity is emphasized by architecture rather than decoration, and experience, history and thought resonate beneath every surface. A low-profile plinth on the opposite wall mirrors the shape of the desk base and serves as a location for sculptural artwork and corporate literature.

The next 'layer' of the design is a quintet of glass-fronted meeting rooms, arranged on either side of the reception space. At the flip of a switch, the entire floor-to-ceiling expanse of each glass panel can be transformed from transparent to opaque when visual privacy is required. Doorways to each room, are darkly framed to echo the strong geometry of the building's windows. Each meeting room is named after a wine region of France and decorated to match, reflecting the bank's historical French origins and prestige.

The open plan responds to the building's shallow core-to-window depth, with low partitions between workstations ensuring unobstructed sightlines. The workstations repeat the striking 'window frame' motif with dark, well-defined edging, a measure which naturally leads the eye toward the office's actual windows and, inevitably, to the sweeping view of Hong Kong beyond.

Though outwardly a design of immediate simplicity and elegance, close examination of this office's contrasting smooth and hard-edged forms, its distinctive palette of colors, textures and materials, and even the way its spaces are arranged soon reveals a sophistication that lies just below the surface.

Architecture:
M Moser Associates
Client:
Societe Generale

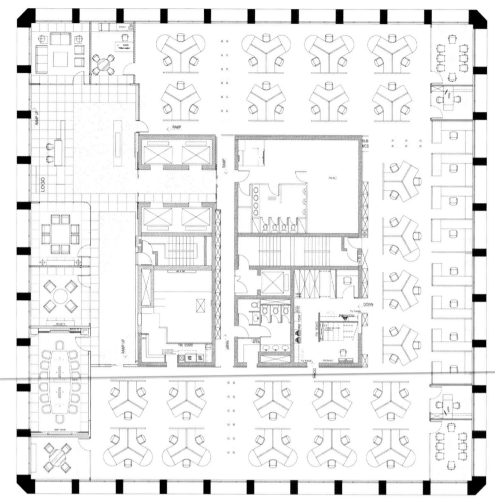

Floor plan

A long and intriguing corporate heritage, a move to utilize space, and making a virtue of architectural necessity gave form to Societe Generale Private Banking's new Hong Kong office.

The reception is on the 38th floor, with the rest of the design radiating out from this 'anchor': meeting rooms follow, and then the back-of-house. These three layers – reception, meeting rooms, back of house-- correspond with the layers of SGPB's business and how it serves its clients. Direct from the lifts, visitors step onto a red carpet whose hue echoes that of SGPB's logo and carries the implication of VIP treatment. The logo is rendered nearby in a subtle imprint on the wall.

CHAMPAGNE

Stephen Williams Associates

Jung von Matt Advertising Agency

Hamburg, Germany   **Photographs:** contributed by Stephen Williams Associates

In 2010, the agency group Jung von Matt commissioned Stephen Williams Associates to extend one of their offices in Hamburg's trendy "Karolinenviertel" by two floors to accommodate the agency management and the accounting department. Jung von Matt now occupies the entire 19th century factory building.

Agency heavyweights have a new home on the fourth floor, and now reside in a space that was quickly dubbed the "elephant house". Stephen Williams Associates designed a communal executive's office that indeed bears some similarities to one. There is only one huge table which all directors share which sits heavily in the middle of an otherwise sparsely furnished room dominated by the use of strong and dark materials. Two small cabins in the corners, the "quiet rooms", offer the only opportunity to retreat. Stationery and personal items are kept in custom-built containers that strongly resemble feeding troughs. The management assistants sit across the hallway – they share offices in twos and keep an eye on the individuals in their care through a hefty steel and glass enclosure.

The experience of sitting in the staff café, located on the same floor, is meant to suggest that of being on the inside of the Trojan horse, the agency's famous logo. It is an entirely wood-clad, comfortable space for informal conversations over a tea or coffee, which the client recognizes so often provide the spark for big ideas. A reference to the Trojan horse is also found on the first floor, which provides new offices for the accounting department. The communal area, a long, stretched, open corridor, accommodates everything from dog houses and copy machines to meeting tables in a furniture sculpture that can easily be interpreted as the track of the Trojan horse, the structure needed to keep it going – much like the accounting to the agency.

In close contact with Jung von Matt's management, Stephen Williams Associates has succeeded in finding a timeless design that reflects the agency's character and idiosyncrasies in every detail. What at first glance seems an unusual setup, the "elephant house," was developed with a keen understanding of the client's unconventional and radical approach. The minimal elements in the room free its users from the unnecessary and encourages communication and focus. One of the company's main principles to themselves fresh is to be self-critical and to "remain dissatisfied." With the work of the designers, however, they are for once more than satisfied.

Architecture:
Stephen Williams Associates

Client:
Jung von Matt, advertising agency

Area:
1,600 sqm (17,200 sqft)

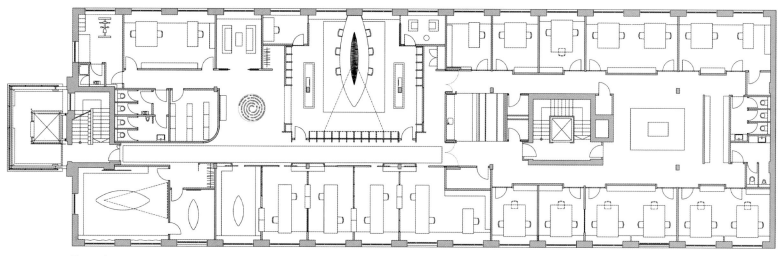

Floor plan

The communal area, a long, stretched, open corridor, accommodates everything from dog houses and copy machines to meeting tables in a furniture sculpture that can easily be interpreted as the track of the Trojan horse, the structure needed to keep it going – much like the accounting to the agency.

There is only one huge table which all directors share which sits heavily in the middle of an otherwise sparsely furnished room dominated by the use of strong and dark materials. Two small cabins in the corners, the "quiet rooms", offer the only opportunity to retreat.

The experience of sitting in the staff café, located on the same floor, is meant to suggest that of being on the inside of the Trojan horse, the agency's famous logo.

Ippolito Fleitz Group - Identity Architects

schlaich bergermann und partner headquarters

Stuttgart, Germany

Photographs: Zooey Braun

schlaich bergermann und partner is an engineering firm with a global reputation, known above all for its stadiums, bridges and energy concepts. The firm has offices in Berlin, New York and São Paulo in addition to its main company headquarters in Stuttgart. The Stuttgart team of 110 employees used to be based in two different locations. The relocation of the entire company to a fully redeveloped, seven-story office block dating from the 1970s pursued the goal of reuniting the team under one roof. The building is prominently located at a busy crossroads in the urban district of West Stuttgart.

The first and largest floor houses the communicative heart of the company, consisting of reception, a meeting place, a bistro and conference space. This is where all the meeting rooms and the administrative and organizational divisions are located. A wide range of seating situations offers different ambiences and the right setting for every kind of discussion. The idea is that communication should not only take place during break times but should be an integral part of the everyday workflow.

Visitors ascend to the first floor via a free-floating staircase engineered by the company itself. It leads to the reception area, from which the space opens up in a choreographed manner. The first section of the room is flanked by an aluminum wall, inset with black magnetic strips creating presentation surfaces. Behind the reception is a first row of desks for back office and administrative tasks. The reception desk is also the starting point for a strip of carpet laid on the mineral-coated concrete. Indentations in the carpet have a signpost function and point to the different functional zones within the space. A 17 meter-long lighting strip suspended from the ceiling is both a beam of light and an additional means of orientation. A spacious communication area forms the centerpiece of this floor. Its generous dimensions signal the importance in which this communal communicative space is held. It is contained beneath a punched metal ceiling that serves an additional acoustic purpose. Individual zones below offer varied settings for differing communicative requirements. The neon green dots on the floor are designed to conjure up associations of a meadow, thus building a conceptual bridge to the terrace, which is delineated by a green wall at one end.

Each floor consists of a varying number of individual offices and separate teamwork areas, as well as a large open-plan work space. The glass façades of the individual offices run along two longitudinal axes, and are positioned differently on each floor. The result is one of varied spatial landscapes. Yet the continuous glass façades of the single offices still render them optically accessible and thus part of the overall space.

Architecture:
Ippolito Fleitz Group - Identity Architects
Client:
sbp GmbH
Team:
Peter Ippolito, Gunter Fleitz, Tilla Goldberg,
Christian Kirschenmann, Jakub Pakula,
Stefanie Maurer, Sherief Sabet,
Markus Schmidt, Daniela Schröder
Area:
2,500 sqm (26,900 sqft)

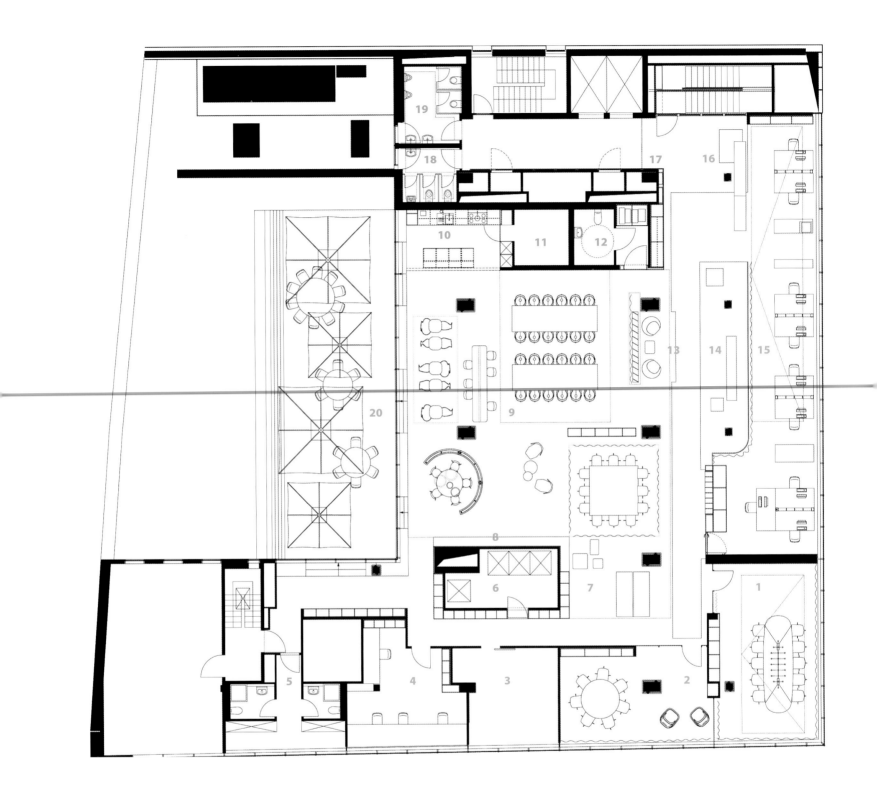

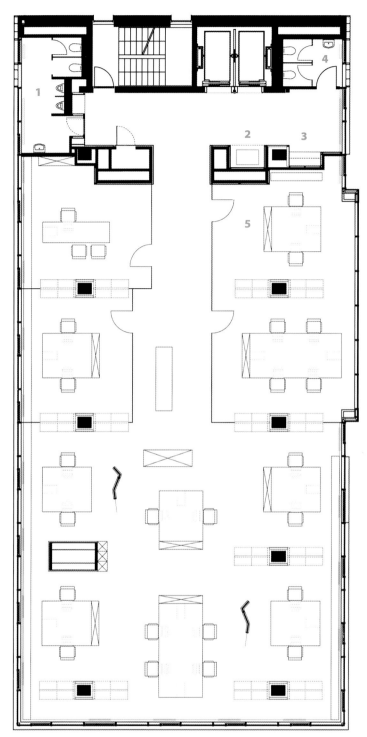

Visitors ascend to the first floor via a free-floating staircase engineered by the company itself. It leads to the reception area, from which the space opens up in a choreographed manner.

A spacious communication area forms the centerpiece of this floor. Its generous dimensions signal the importance in which this communal communicative space is held. It is contained beneath a punched metal ceiling that serves an additional acoustic purpose.

The glass façades of the individual offices run along two longitudinal axes, and are positioned differently on each floor. The result is one of varied spatial landscapes. Yet the continuous glass façades of the single offices still render them optically accessible and thus part of the overall space.

id+s Design Solutions

THQ Studio

Montréal, Canada

Photographs: Claude-Simon Langlois

In 2012 Montreal design firm id+s Design Solutions won the Grands Prix du Design award for Office Design excellence across Quebec (for 20,000 sqft and over) for the offices of THQ, an American developer and publisher of video games.

THQ, a multi-national video games company, opened their largest development studio in Montreal in 2010, occupying 5,300 sqm (57,000 sqft) on 2 floors in a historic building: the former headquarters and printing press of the Montréal Gazette newspaper.

This massive studio with a 400–person capacity includes multiple disciplines that serve as THQ's creative engine. The client's objective was to maximize the number of people in a collaborative workplace setting and social zones.

The large floor plates were divided into 2 distinctive zones: a darker atmosphere was designated for the artists, a brighter outdoor setting in honeycomb-shaped workstations and wooden "skate park" platforms, for the other disciplines.

Over-sized metal poles feed the electrical and communication cabling, and create an abstraction of trees or lampposts. Connecting these 2 zones is a giant-sized white tunnel incorporating social gathering spaces and offices.

Complementary rooms take on a theme of their own; the lunchroom turns into an outdoor rest stop, the screening room exposes its theatrical side and conference room tables transform themselves into ping-pong tables.

The space emulates the very nature of the organization, each zone plays out as series of screen shots underscoring the culture of the multi-media industry, work at play. It is another triumph for id+s design solutions, a multi-disciplinary team of 12 designers and technicians of acknowledged merit.

Architecture:
id+s Design Solutions Inc.
Project leader:
Susie Silveri
Design team:
Stefania Pasto, Pascale Fouchard
Architect:
Réal Paul
Engineers:
Bouthillette Parizeau
Surface area:
5,300 sqm (57, 000 sqft)

The space emulates the very nature of the organization, each zone plays out as series of screen shots underscoring the culture of the multi-media industry, work at play.

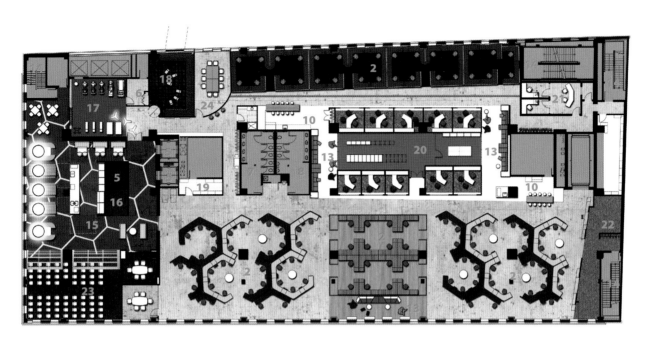

Upper floor plan

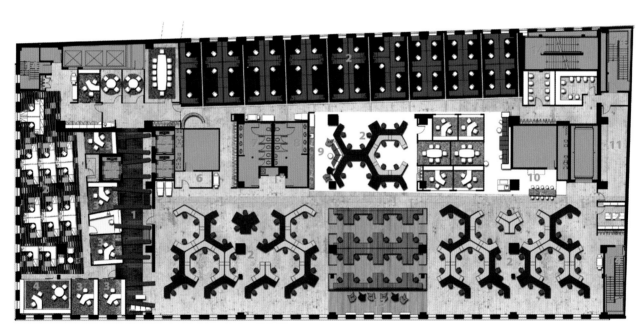

Lower floor plan

KEY

1. Reception	6. Storage	11. Compatibility Lab &	15. Lunch room	20. Server room
2. Working stations	7. Women toilets	Mastering Lab	16. Pantry	21. Audio studio
3. Manager room	8. Men toilets	12. Storage	17. Fitness center	22. Scrum room
4. General manager room	9. Kitchen lounge	13. Lounge	18. Screening room	23. Training room
5. Elevator	10. Coffee area	14. Staircases	19. Library - secure	24. Conference room

Complementary rooms take on a theme of their own; the lunchroom turns into an outdoor rest stop, the screening room exposes its theatrical side and conference room tables transform themselves into ping-pong tables.